The Official Veterinary Marketing Guide

How to Use Online Media, Viral Marketing
and Direct Response to Grow Your
Veterinary Practice in today's Economy

Jonathan Taylor

Russell Portwood

First Printing, 2011

Printed in the United States of America

The Official Veterinary Marketing Guide

How to Use Online Media, Viral Marketing and Direct Response to Grow Your Veterinary Practice in today's Economy

Table of Contents

Introduction

Once upon a time, long ago, life was simpler. Business was simpler. An entrepreneur could place a few local ads, hang an *open for business* sign on the storefront door and wait for customers to come streaming in. But times have changed. (Was it really that long ago?)

You as a veterinarian in the 21st century must change with the times if you want your business to survive. It is no longer just enough to be a good doctor; you need to be so much more. You must be a savvy marketer who understands the benfits of viral marketing, social media, blogs and podcasting. The electronic age touches everything we do now. And it changes. Fast.

The internet has changed the way companies everywhere are communicating with customers. It's no longer enough to run a large yellow page ad with your clinics phone number in bold print. Fewer and fewer people are flipping through the pages of the yellow book when they need a good veterinarian. Instead, they are going to Google.

 It is increasingly difficult to compete for your future client's attention in the current world we live in. Or your present client's for that matter. Getting the message of your clinic out while cutting through the clutter can be overwhelming and expensive for someone without the skill of a stealth marketer. But without it there are fewer and fewer new clients. Plus, you face the danger of your existing clients getting drawn away by the more tech savvy vets. And what about the older clients who prefer that things really shouldn't change? How do you deal with it all?

Direct client referrals are wonderful and vital to a clinic but they are not adequate enough to support healthy and sustainable growth. Internal and external marketing that cuts through the clutter is no longer optional but a must. The irony of the newer electronic marketing methods becomes evident when the impersonal nature of the internet becomes split-second one-on-one with the likes of Twitter, Facebook, and other developing social interfaces. People carry the internet around with them in their pockets now. Think about that.

A common problem in the veterinary industry as with other industries is what is called "marketing incest". One veterinarian sees what another is doing and simply copies it without really knowing if it truly works (which most of the time it doesn't). It's really the blind leading the blind. While this may sound a little discouraging, it places the astute vet who knows about marketing, in a position to stand out from the rest of the crowd and succeed at really growing their practice. You can be that success story. It's not that hard but the proper foundation is necessary. Building on what is truly important in any business and then using the proper tools to reach and satisfy clients may not be simple but it doesn't have to take up so much time as to be a frustration.

Wouldn't a roadmap be nice? Especially considering the road keeps moving? Welcome to marketing in the new century.

This book, *The Official Veterinary Marketing Guide,* can be that roadmap. You already have the foundation: quality care, personal service, and a professional approach to one of the most important disciplines in the lives of people and their animal companions. This part is solid. But the marketing aspect is more fluid and you need to adjust to the changing nature of attracting and keeping clients. What you need to do is build a *system* that adjusts to the changes. The system will follow the appropriate map to assure you don't have an empty waiting room. Once again your focus is on quality care and client satisfaction as you build a thriving practice.

Obviously, every veterinary practice is different. Yours has a personality all its own. It has your touch. Your clients know you and trust you to care for their pets. Just as you have built that foundation of care, you can build a foundation for your marketing efforts as well – even if the business landscape keeps changing. Use the information in this book to customize a strategy unique to your practice and then, once your system is in place, you will only have to make minor adjustments but the foundation will stand firm. This small investment in time now will pay large dividends over the coming years.

Thank you for allowing us to be a part of your success. We sincerely appreciate it!

If you would like a Free 30 minute marketing consultation on how to grow your veterinary practice using the strategies in this book call us at 866-724-0355 or visit our website at www.VetNetMarketing.com and fill out the contact form.

Chapter 1
Marketing Your Vet Practice Online

The BIG Difference in This Recession

In contrast to the last recession in the early 90s, this current downturn has an additional potential savior – the Internet. Used well, the Internet can be your recessionary life raft to provide you with an effective way to outsmart outmarket and outperform your competitors.

Fortunately, not many veterinarians know how to use the Internet as a powerful tool to really effectively market their product or service. Sure, a lot of businesses are throwing money towards marketing themselves online but most of them are not doing it that well at all. We can help you to change that.

But first of all, why should you even consider using the Internet to help you and your veterinary practice to survive and even thrive in this recession and beyond?

4 Major Reasons to Market Online
Here are 4 major reasons why the Internet should be a significant part of your overall marketing strategy:

Reason # 1: People Are Spending MORE Money Online
According to a comScore research report, the number of people actually searching for products and services online increased by 21% in 2008.

So the Internet is a growing trend and more and more of your propects and customers likely to look for you online.
Why?

It's convenient and a great way for them to save time and often save money too. Remember that a lot of people are time-poor in today's hectic 24/7 society.

Having more people searching for your product and service is one thing. The important question is: are they spending more money online?

A comScore study reported that US e-commerce spending in 2010 reached a staggering $227.6 billion – a 9% increase over the previous year. So importantly, more people are spending more money online too – they're not just lookie-loos and information seekers.

They've got cash to spend and they're going to spend it online somewhere the only question is: will it be with you or your competitors? And the most popular search engine?

As you can see in the following pie chart, Google is the most popular and significant search engine – by far.

The comScore study revealed that the top 5 search engines were Google, Yahoo!, Microsoft, Ask and AOL. Google gets 66% - two thirds – of all searches in the US. Yahoo! gets 16% of the searchers, with Microsoft, Ask and AOL scrambling for most of the scraps. To get the most exposure, focus your efforts on Google and then Yahoo! if you have the resources.

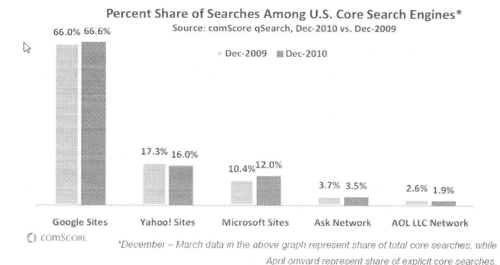

Percent Share of Searches Among U.S. Core Search Engines*
Source: comScore qSearch, Dec-2010 vs. Dec-2009

*December – March data in the above graph represent share of total core searches, while April onward represent share of explicit core searches.

Where does your company website appear on Google for the typical phrases that your prospects and customers are searching for? If your company website doesn't appear, you're effectively invisible and don't exist on the Internet. We can help you to greatly increase the visibility and sales for your business online.

Reason # 2: If You Don't, Your Competitors Get the Profits

Chances are good that your competitors have already realized the benefits of marketing their business online. So if you don't have a significant online presence then you're losing out on the Internet visitors and they will go to your competitors instead – together with their money now and most likely into the future too.

Fortunately, most businesses that are marketing themselves on the Internet are doing a mediocre job at best and can usually be easily beaten online – with some correctly applied expertise.

Reason # 3: Online = Greater Return on Investment

As marketing budgets come under more pressure, businesses are now looking for methods that have a proven return-on-investment (ROI) so that they can get more bang from their marketing bucks. Because of this, a lot of businesses are using online marketing methods such as e-mail marketing and search engine marketing which are proven to outperform traditional media such as advertising.

But where should you spend your marketing dollars online?
Well, a Sapient survey in 2007 found that 38% of online marketers ranked online search as their #1 marketing channel for providing ROI with e-mail marketing second at 24% and digital advertising at 15%. According to a study by the Direct Marketing Association, the ROI from email marketing in 2008 was $45.06 for every dollar spent while direct offline marketing had an ROI of just $15.55 for ever dollar invested. (Source: The Power of Direct Marketing Economic Study 2008 by the Direct Marketing Association).

In yet another study by McKinsey of 340 senior marketing executives in June 2008, they found that 91% were using online advertising and over half said that they plan to maintain or increase their current online spend. More importantly, 55% said that they are cutting expenditure on traditional media to be able to increase their online efforts.
So, the trend is for savvy businesses to shift their marketing dollars from traditional offline methods such as advertising to online methods that have greater ROI.

Reason # 4: Online Marketing Influences Offline Sales

One of the key things to understand is that people's buying behavior has changed as a direct result of the Internet. People are increasingly likely to do a search for a product or service online and then either purchase it online there and then or use it later to influence their purchasing decisions once they do go offline.

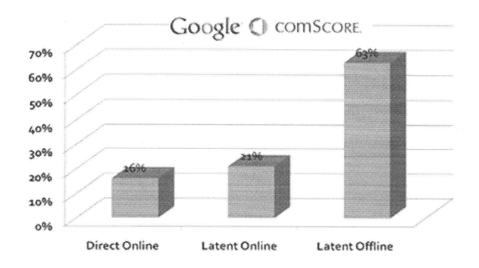

A joint Google and comScore study on "The Role of Search in Consumer Buying" found that immediate online sales accounted for only 16% of activity and a further 21% of sales came online at some point later after the search. More strikingly, a whopping 63% of sales came from activity done offline at some point after the online search was conducted.

(The study was conducted in March 2006 and examined activity across 11 product categories over a 60-day period).

This holds true for business-to-business sales as well as just business-to-consumer sales. For example, in their Business to Business survey of 2007, Enquiro discovered that 36.4% of respondents found vendors online but then completed their purchase offline later. (Source: Enquiro "Business to Business Survey 2007" May 2007)

So, the buying decisions of your prospects and clients are being greatly influenced online and will lead to offline sales. If you are not there to influence them online, then they'll most likely not buy from you when they go looking for the services of a good veterinarian offline as well.

We can help you to increase your online presence so that online prospects and clients find your veterinary practice instead of your competitor.

The Internet is breaking down the barriers of communication to the public. Veterinarians can now get their message out without spending a fortune. Today's economic times are causing many small business owners to rethink how they spend their marketing and advertising dollars.

This book will teach you, as a veterinarian, to implement these new strategies of Marketing and PR. Most cost little to nothing. The new tactical weapons of promotion include:

- Autoresponders
- Blogging
- Content Rich Sites
- Podcasting
- Video Marketing
- Social Media

The point of teaching you all of these is to get you implementing them all together. Don't count on just one alone. Implement or find someone to implement all of these if possible. Using New Marketing Media, a veterinarian can dominate their local market.

During tough economic times, it's even more essential to implement new online technologies. Here's the problem—almost all veterinarians are doing the same thing when it comes to marketing.

They buy a yellow page ad that looks about the same as every other. Some actually do have their own Web site, but it's usually nothing more than a boring brochure posted online.

What if, however, you ran across that one exceptional veterinarian who stood apart from all the rest? You know the one that has his or her own online YouTube channel that featured weekly "Pet Care Tips". The one that also has a weekly show on BlogTalkRadio where they discuss proper nutrition for your dog or cat. This veterinarian might also have a website offering a free special report, "The 7 Things You Can Do to

Keep Your Dog Health and Happy" just for signing up for their weekly newsletter and updates.You'd start to notice that this veterinarian is doing something completely different from most. This person has branded themselves as the qualified go-to expert.

New marketing is not about using one single online tool. It's about using a combination of web technologies that will promote your practice virally. It's about using permission marketing to connect with your existing clients.

As author Seth Godin describes it, permission marketing is the privilege (not the right) of delivering anticipated personal and relevant messages to people who actually want to get them. It's about creating a written or video blog that educates your customers about your industry. It's about an online radio show. How relevant are social networking sites to your business? If you're not implementing these strategies into your own veterinarian practice, visit www.VetnetMarketing.com to find out how we cazn help you.

Chapter 2

Website Strategies: Content is King

Statistics show that the majority of people only stay thirty seconds at any given site before clicking away. If that's the case, then you've got to have something to entice them to stay longer. A site that tells people who you are and how long you've been in business is not going to keep people interested. Let me be clearer—it's just plain boring.

In order to get prospects to stay, you have to provide good information that will keep them clicking from one link to another all through your site. "Content is king", as they say in online marketing. You need to have articles or videos related to your industry that people can download.

As a veterinarian, your site should be loaded with valuable content that keeps your visitors coming back again and again. Let me give you an example. *Barger and Sons*, a local water and sewer services company where we live, has a page on their Web site titled "learning center." If you click on the link you'll find a wealth of articles, white papers, and videos on everything you might need or want to know about septic tanks and grease traps.

I'm sure that may not sound very interesting, but if you ever get a backed-up system, you'll want to know all about what's going on and how to prevent the problem next time. A local wine store that I purchase from has a Web site that features an "Easy Wine Reference Section." The page has links to information like "wine tasting basics" and "wine and food pairing." These sections contain a few short articles, but imagine what they could do if they followed the example of Gary Vaynerchuck's Wine Library TV (tv.winelibrary.com). They could have a video of the week on how to pair wine up with food, or a "wine tasting for dummies" for people who want to learn from the experts.

The same is true for the veterinarian industry. As consultants, we specialize in helping veterinarians develop websites that have white paper reports, video and audio tips and other resources that will make potential clients come back again and again.

Differentiate by Offering Good Information

Your web content should be customer focused. Find out what they are interested in.When analyzing your existing site; ask yourself the quetion-"Does it talk about our cutting edge, state of the art products and services or our commitment to total customer satisfaction?" Boring! Phrases like this have been so overused that they start to lose effectiveness over time.

Let's take your average realtor as an example. Any real-estate agent can tell you on their Web site how committed they are to getting your house sold. That should be a given. That doesn't impress me. What would impress me is a realtor who offers incredible value up front. They might have a mortgage calculator on their site to help me figure out monthly payments.

They might have a page on their site that shows average real-estate prices in certain areas of their state. They might even have a free downloadable ebook on the "The 7 secrets To Getting Your House Sold Quickly Even in a Down Market." or an audio report on "5 Simple Ways to Improve the Value of Your Home." Their site might even have a link to a blog that features the latest news on the housing market.We'll talk about how to set up an effective blog in the next chapter. If they don't want to write out lengthy reports, they could use video or audio content for their site.

One realtor in San Diego does just that. With a pocket camcorder, Jim Klinge takes video of houses that are overpriced. He points out the flaws of each one, and explains why they aren't worth the asking price. In one video, he walks in and shows the inside of a house where the previous owners had stolen the decorative pillars off the wall. He laughs,"They took the pillars!" He posts these videos to his Web site (www.bubbleinfo.com), which gets about two thousand hits a day.This realtor is what Jay Conrad Levinson, author of the book Guerrilla Marketing, calls a Guerrilla marketer.

By posting this information to his blog site, he is positioning himself as an advocate for the buyer—a realtor who's looking out for people who've gotten ripped off in the past. He's getting plenty of buyers when other realtors are getting out of the business.

Jim Klinge's guerrilla tactic is just one example of how content can spread.Videos can be picked up and shared with others all over the web. His videos are uploaded to YouTube and then posted on his site. People can view them and share them by visiting his YouTube channel and clicking the "share" link.

His video can then be shared with others on MySpace, Facebook, or Twitter. Not only that, the video code can be picked up by others and embedded on other Web sites, making it viral.

As a veterinarian, you can create content that's useful and spreads. You can post articles on free online directories like EzineArticles.com a Goarticles.com. These sites allow you to write articles on topics related to your field of expertise. At the end of each article, you can post a link in the signature box that directs people back to your site. Here is a list of the top twenty article directories:

- Ezinearticles.com
- Buzzle
- SearchWarp
- GO Articles
- Article Alley
- Article Dash Board
- Web Pro News
- Article Click
- Amazines
- Article Nexus
- Idea Marketers
- Articles Sphere
- Articles Factory
- Article-Buzz
- Article Depot
- Article Garden
- Artilces Natch
- Article City
- Upublish

There are also article submitter software programs that allow you to submit your articles to a number of article directories at one time. One that's very popular among many article writers can be found at www.articlesubmitterpro.com.

You might even want to hire it out using a virtual assistant. If you offer written reports or ebooks on your site, you want to make sure you insert links through this information that directs people back to website.

Obviously, you're giving away free information, but you want that information leading them to the ultimate solution of their pet's health problems—you!

The information you provide on your site should be focused on educating and bringing value, but don't forget that your job is to position yourself as the primary solution to your customer's needs. <u>Explain to them how you'll solve their greatest problem.</u>

Another great example of this is the carpet cleaner whose report describes all the creepy parasites that get trapped in your carpet. I can see this carpet cleaner having a site where he posts videos of some of the most disgusting-looking carpet that he's had to clean.

Using Online PR

If you have newsworthy content on your site, you can utilize online PR sites like PRweb.com and PRnewswire.com. We often use PRweb with our clients because of the affordable cost per press release.

I'm reminded of the guys who gained national attention by showing off the chemical effect of dropping Mentos candy into a bottle of Diet Coke. Their videos spread like wildfire across the web, getting them picked up by news outlets, and finally a spot on the David Letterman Show.

News outlets are always eager for exciting content that may be timely or unique. You'll need to submit a press release in order to get picked up.

Here are a few guidelines for writing an effective press release:
- Make it newsworthy. Don't try to promote your service directly. If it sounds like an advertisement for your service, it probably won't get picked up.
- Use a captivating headline that gets attention.
- Use illustrations of how your service has helped solve a problem with one of your clients. Give a real life story (not an advertisement).
- Relate it to current events. One of the biggest news items right now is the economy. What is your veterinary clinic doing to help others during slow economic times?

- Make it unique. If you're launching a new product or service, you'll need some unique spin on it. There are plenty of new product launches going on all the time. What's different about yours? Think about Jim the realtor. He's doing something different. You should be too in your veterinary practice.

One successful news release can generate tens of thousands of visitors to your site in one day. You certainly want to be prepared for the traffic you start getting. This leads us right in to our next section.

Start a Blog for Your Veterinary Practice

There are more than 150,000 blogs created every day. Many are just a means for people to rant or communicate with friends and family, but blogs can be an effective marketing tool for a number of reasons. They are a great way to build enormous trust with your customers. A blog is an open forum that lets you communicate what's going on and, at the same time, lets your customers give feedback. It's also a way of building your reputation as the go-to expert in your industry. The more you write, the more attention you gain.

Let me give you a short example of the power of a blog in building your reputation as an expert. Few people would have known who Jon Ostrower was just a few years ago. But that changed when he started blogging about the latest updates on the development of the Boeing 787. Ostrower had no aerospace training; neither did he have a background in journalism.

All he really had was a serious interest in what he was writing about. His readership, which started out at only 315, grew to well over 1.7 million. His status grew as well. His reputation as the inside man on the 787 landed him a job writing for the trade journal *Flight International*.

Blogs are very powerful. They give you a channel that your audience can access easily. If you post entries on a regular basis, include your blog address on any other printed materials you have such as business cards or brochures. If you post often enough and if your blogs are informative, people will begin to subscribe so that they get automated updates every time you post.

Get Your Employees Involved

In your own vet practice, you can get your employees to blog. This might make some owners a little nervous, but it's a great way to create an open forum with your customer base. Obviously, guidelines will need to be set as to what they should be posting, but you do want them to be able to express ideas or solutions to customer complaints.

Blogs are a great way to share testimonials from some of your satisfied clients. Blogging is simply a way of putting a face on your company. Your customers like to see some personality behind a name.

Creating a Remarkable Blog

Anyone can get a free blog started using WordPress or Blogger. You can set an account up with either of these services and begin blogging in about five minutes. I recommend, however, having a blog uploaded onto your hosting account. This still costs nothing if you already have a host provider with your current site.

The barrier to overcome is learning how to do it. You can find some helpful training videos on how to install and setup a blog at www.VetNetMarketing.com. If you simply don't have the time to do it, don't let that hold you back. Our team of web designers and marketers at *VetNet Marketing* can create a customized blog for your vet practice in about 2-3 days.

Chapter 3
Email Marketing

Using Permission Marketing to Build a Long Term Relationship with Clients

One of the most under-utilized tools in marketing today with most small businesses is direct response by email, or what author Seth Godin has termed "Permission Marketing". As I mentioned previously, permission marketing is offering useful content that people want. This can be accomplished through frequent email updates, such as weekly news, tips, or even specials that your vet practice might be running.

I recently visited a local tire and service center to get my vehicle inspected. I could tell just from talking to the manager that business was down. Yet when I went to pay for the service, they never asked for my email address to send out sales promotions.

I would have been happy to give it to them, but they apparently didn't see the value. Talk about wasted chances! It was a missed opportunity to put my information into a database so that they could send out email coupons for oil changes, tire rotations, or tune-ups. Think of all the possiblilities of having me as a customer on an email list.

I thought that maybe the employee that I paid just forgot to ask, so I checked their Web site. There was no opt-in box where I could sign up for an e-newsletter. What I found was nothing more than what I like to call a "brochure site"—a site that tells you *Who We Are*, *How Long We've Been in Business*, and *How You Can Contact Us*.

Sadly, this is still the format that so many businesses are using for their Web sites. They allow IT guys or friends who know nothing about direct marketing to create their Web site. Very big mistake! It's costing them money every day.

Similarly most veterinarian websites have no opt-in email form on their home page. Implementing an email auto-responder into your marketing plan can begin increasing your revenu from existing clients right away. An email marketing campaign is essential for getting current customers to buy from you over and over again. One of the best systems that I've found is AWeber. You can find them at www.aweber.com.

AWeber is a powerful tool for email marketing. For $19 a month, you can use their online service to host all of your email lists and create newsletters, autoresponders, or RSS to email. This online software allows you to create an opt-in box and then gives you the html code so that you can place it onto your existing Web site. It's really very simple. AWeber also has online screencast tutorials that will teach you everything you need to know.

The opt-in box can be placed within the template of your existing site or show up as a light box over the existing web page. This opt-in form can be customized to ask customers for more than just their name and email address so that you can get other detailed information on them.

AWeber also offers double opt-in, which means that customers who sign up for your email updates will have to confirm that they have indeed requested to be put on your email list campaign. A confirmation link is sent to their email address immediately after they sign up at your Web site. This feature saves you from being accused of spamming.

Once you start getting sign-ups it's important to send them something of value. You don't want to bombard your customers with promotions. This is certainly the fastest way to kill the golden goose. Instead, provide them with a weekly newsletter offering tips or other information that will make them want to read your emails.

If you already have a "pet tips" section on your website, you may want to take this information and use it in your email newsletters as well. At the end of each newsletter, you might place a special discount coupon that's only good for one week. This is not only a great way to bring customers in more frequently, but also a great way to educate them and provide something of value at the same time.

Part of our consulting services at VetNet Marketing include helping veterinarians establish effective email marketing campaigns for their websites.

Giving Something of Value

As we mentioned, in order to get people to sign up for your email newsletter, you should offer them something of value. Simply offering to send them email updates on your latest specials often times won't cut it. People get enough junk email everyday, so the last thing they want is extra stuff to delete.

That's why we recommend a tip-of-the-week email; something that educates your customer. Also, you can offer a free report that they might find useful and informative. A free report could be something that you write (or have someone else write) that offers a solution or provides some education.

Power of One - Singleness of Purpose

In order to get visitors to sign up for your email campaign, you really need to be focused on the objective. What I mean by that is letting them know what you want them to do as soon as they come to your site. If your opt-in box is hidden out of sight, or is crowded in with the other links on your navigation menu, then it's very likely most people won't even notice.Your objective is to make things clear. For many sites, having a simple landing page is the best way to go.

A landing page is nothing more than a simple one page site that instructs the visitor what you want them to do, which of course is to sign up for your email newsletter.

After they sign up on the landing page, you can then have them directed to the main Web site that has all of the company info. Another option is to implement a "light box" on your existing site. A light box is like a pop-up ad, but far less annoying.The opt-in box simply fades in after you been on the site for a few seconds.

The Real Value in Email Marketing
The biggest advantage to using direct response email is that it gets your current clients coming back for your services again and again. The biggest mistake that most veterinarians make is wasting their advertising dollars on trying to get new customers. The truth is, it takes twice as much effort to get a new prospect to buy from you than it does for a client who's purchased from you in the past. It amazes me just how few businesses realize this.

Some restaurants use this strategy by printing a message on their receipts offering weekly coupons to customers who sign up at their Web site. Moe's Southwest Grill is a great example of this. If you visit their site, you can sign up for news, special promotions, and even a birthday gift. They realize that it's ultimately about keeping faithful customers coming back again and again.

Plus using email marketing is easier and cheaper than advertising. The real value is long-term relationships that will continue on for years as you communicate with them.

Chapter 4
Social Media Marketing:

Using the Power of Social Media Sites to Gain More Loyal Clients to Your Practice

When it comes to marketing, the veterinary industry tends to be stuck in a rut. The same marketing tools are used over and over again, without much thought as to how well they are performing. If you think that those reminder cards that you send and your yellow page ads are the answer, then you are overlooking a tremendous opportunity.

Your yellow page ad is a great example. Depending on your geographic location, you could spend anywhere from a few hundred dollars a month, to thousands of dollars per month advertising your business. Yet, yellow page ads offer you very little return on your investment. The world has moved on.

The definition of Veterinary Marketing has changed dramatically in the last few years. Replacing the traditions of long ago, new dynamic strategies are both affordable for the small business and deliver results. Change is difficult, but embracing the need for it will put you miles ahead of your competition.

Social media marketing is the process of promoting your veterinary practice through social media channels, such as Digg, Twitter, or Facebook. Although this is a relatively new concept for Veterinarians, it can be a powerful, low cost promotional tool to promote your practice online. As the popularity of these sites continues to grow, there has never been a better time for mastering the techniques of successful social media marketing.

Veterinarians who are not on the social media bandwagon generally have mixed feelings about these sites. Either they do not understand it, or they do not believe in the value that it can bring to a Veterinary Practice. Yet, the fact remains that there are many success stories from other industries that used Social media to catapult their business form mediocre to outstanding.

Dell Computers is a great case study. When Dell created their "Outlet", which sells re furbished computers, they opted to promote their product using the online social media resource "Twitter". They have developed their site to not only make people aware of deals, but to encourage customer feedback and form relationships with the customers. Are you wondering how well social media marketing really works? To date, Dell has booked over $3 Million in revenue from its Twitter posts alone. Imagine the implications if that success is multiplied over mutiple social media sites!

Benefits of Social Media Marketing
The benefits of social media marketing are multi-fold. It is an evolving process used to build your practice over time; it is not a quick way to generate income. The good news is that while it may take a while, it cost virtually nothing. If done by yourself, expenditure is limited to zilch but your time. You would spend thousands of dollars in advertising to gain the same exposure that these sites will give you for nothing. While that is a huge benefit in itself, here are a few others worth considering.

- Benefit #1: Improve your search engine ranking through links. These sites allow you to establish "links" to your website. The more sites that you have linking to your website, the higher your search engine ranking will be. In a sense, you are borrowing the trust and authority of big sites to boost your own rank. This will increase the amount of traffic that visits you.
- Benefit # 2: Increased primary and secondary traffic will lead to increased popularity. Regardless of how much time people spend on your website, you need traffic in order to promote your practice. Primary traffic comes from direct links through the social media sites to your site. Secondary traffic occurs when blogs or other sites link to content on your social media page. Both types of traffic are valuable, because they provide you with the opportunity to educate

your current clients and get potential new clients to "subscribe" to your newsletter.

- Benefit #3: Your website is exposed to large groups of people that are actually interested in your services. This provides you with a limitless audience in which to market to, free of charge.

For example, imagine that you want to spread the word about your dental promotion. You could try writing an article titled "Your Pet's Health May Be at Risk! Learn the One Simple Thing You Can Do to Prevent Heart, Lung, and Kidney Disease in Your Best Friend".

Include useful information on how important dental cleanings are and how it will keep peoples pets healthy. Publish the article on your social media site, and your blog, or someone else's pet related blog. Include a promotion on your website that offers clients an incentive to book a dental prophy with you.

Not only will you generate leads from potential new clients, but your existing clients will get the message also. This type of marketing is easy for anyone to do. Once you have learned the basics, you can immediately put this strategy to work for your practice. There is no secret to mastering the art of social media; anyone and everyone is invited to the party and can participate.

Social Media Websites

- Twitter
- Facebook
- MySpace
- Stumbleupon
- Yelp
- delicious
- LinkedIn

> "... Social media technologies are changing the way that individuals and companies are forming their opinions and buying decisions, even how often they buy."

How does peer influence impact buying habits? According to a recent study of consumer behavior, performed in partnership with iModerate Research Technologies, it was discovered that consumers are "67%

more likely to buy from brands they follow on Twitter, and 51% more likely to buy from a brand they follow on Facebook." This has tremendous implications for the future of marketing your Veterinary Practice.

Do You Tweet?

Twitter is a social networking site that uses text messages (called "Tweets") and micro blogging to connect people with similar interests to each other. The most recent numbers indicate that there are over 14 million users in the United States alone. That number is expected to grow to 18 million in the next couple of years.

Twitter is ranked as one of the top 50 most popular sites. The huge database of people is free to use, and you can easily search for your existing clients to see who is using Twitter. You can then "follow" them, and they can choose to "follow" you. In this manner, you are able to develop a strong network of contacts that you can deliver your message to.

The primary advantage of Twitter is that it allows you to Tweet via your mobile phone, so you do not have to be in front of a computer. Messages are limited to 140 characters. Here are a few suggestions for using Twitter to promote your Veterinary Practice.

1. Promote your Brand. When you use a social networking site to promote your brand, your clients will perceive you as approachable. Stay in touch with your followers and tweet often to reach as many clients and potential clients as possible. Share important pet care tips and facts that are relevant to your client's interests.
2. Consider receiving customer complaints. Although this may seem like a crazy idea, by receiving customer complaints in an open forum, you are able to shut them down before they can damage your reputation. Address them immediately and show everyone how great you customer service is by your attempts at reconciliation with the complainer.
3. Run your special deals and promotions. This is highly effective, especially when combined with a short informative article about the service you are promoting. Try to create a pet health alert bulletin that you use to educate clients about why your services are beneficial.

4. Use it to communicate with your employees. By discussing cases and ongoing patient care with your employees on Twitter, it will allow all of your followers to learn more about what you do.
5. Create credibility by sharing your expertise. If you hold workshops or educational seminars you can Tweet about those to increase awareness. By demonstrating your knowledge, you will build credibility in the eyes of your online community.

Creating Client Connections

Twitter is also a great way to build lasting relationships with your clients. By encouraging feedback, you will not only foster trust, but also learn about how your clients perceive your practice. Always ask for honest feedback and address issues right away. Be sure to communicate any "fixes" that you have instituted and thank your followers for participating.

Think of it as a free platform for everyone, including you, to learn more about how you can improve your Veterinary Practice. Many large companies such as Starbucks, Jet Blue, and Home Depot practice this type of customer support successfully.

You never have to be in the dark about your Twitter reputation. If you have concerns about what your followers may be saying about you, then there is a handy application called Monitter (www.monitter.com) that will send you alerts whenever someone Tweets about you.
Facebook

Facebook is a social networking site that allows users to create a page about themselves or their business, add friends, and send messages. Creating your own "Page" will give your veterinary hospital an identity. Those who are interested in your page will become "fans", and consequently, all of their friends will see this.

Your following is developed through the popularity of your "news feeds", and the more that people like your page, the faster you will grow. In fact, with over 410 Million users, there is potential for your popularity to spread like wildfire. Several companies, such as Adobe and Dunkin Doughnuts use this technique to promote their businesses. Facebook offers several different types of tools for business users. Polls are used to solicit quick opinions from your clients about services that you already offer, or to determine their interest in services that you are considering adding.

Paid advertising is also available. You are able to create creative ads that specifically target a certain demographic. The application allows you to customize who you want your ad to appear to and how often. It is very similar to Google Adwords, and the cost is per click, or per impression. You are able to see exactly how many people your ad will hit and set a limit for how much you want to spend.

Facebook Connect allows you to integrate your Page with your website. You can retrieve friend information, and post data feeds.

Relate To Followers Using Case Studies

A fantastic way for a veterinary hospital to create a following on Facebook is to post actual case studies and request feedback. You can even attach a promotion or create a contest to encourage a lot of activity. For example, let us say that you had an interesting case of Blastomycosis in a dog that was misdiagnosed at another practice.

You cannot only post information about the case, but also updates on how the treatment is progressing. Link to an article on your website, educate everyone about Blastomycosis symptoms, upload pictures, and create an awareness campaign.

It you make the content heartwarming, instead of mostly clinical, then people will relate to it. Ask people to share their stories about their pets that suffered from this disease.

You will not only become an "expert" in the minds of your followers, but you become their "friend", who is a veterinarian. Offer to answer questions and encourage examinations and office visits for those that need it.

Encourage your staff to contribute content. This can be a very effective way to utilize down time, and they are likely already using Facebook. Once you have learned the basics, Facebook is an easy way to break into social media marketing. With so many free tools available and such a large growing audience, it makes sense to consider promoting your practice this way.

MySpace

Myspace isn't just for kids. Although they cater to an audience in their teens, twenties, and thirties, it can still be a resource for promoting your Veterinary Practice. Myspace is basically a website that allows you to create a webpage about you or your business. Once your page is created, you can then connect it to other people's pages.

There is no limit to the number of friends that you can have on Myspace. In fact, some of the most successful users have millions of friends and have become internet celebrities, being featured on television talk shows!

Since the demographic of Myspace users are younger, you should take the time to project a "hip" image that they will connect with. If you are feeling like you are lacking the "hip" factor, you can always have a younger staff member create this page for you.

In order to make Myspace work, you have to think of it as a social network first, and a marketing tool second. The primary goal of the website is to promote friendships. Post pet friendly bulletins and messages that focus on creating relationships.

Many companies have found success using Myspace for selling. It can be an outstanding marketing tool if it is done well.

StumbleUpon

Although not as popular as Twitter, Facebook, and Myspace, StumbleUpon is a very useful marketing tool for promoting your website. This internet community allows the users to rate websites that are targeted to them based on their interests and friends. There is also a blog. The key to StumbleUpon is that you can generate an enormous amount of links to your website. These links will boost your website rankings whenever someone searches for Veterinary services in your area. This in turn will create more traffic to your website, which is (hopefully) created with the goal of getting clients to book an appointment with you.

They offer both free and paid advertising, and you have the ability to create a profile. Creating content, such as pet health care tips, and articles that are targeted to a pet loving audience is the best way to be noticed. Similar sites are "Digg" and "Reddit".

The Controversial Yelp

Yelp is a site that combines search engine function, business reviews, and social networking. They offer both free and paid services. On Yelp, you create a page for your business, which contains your hours, location, service detail, and photos of your practice.

The site is definitely slanted to be more favorable for the reviewers than it is for the businesses. With paid advertising, you can have your listing appear at the top of the search engine rankings, add more photos, and more information about your practice.

Yelp has come under some bad press in the Veterinary community after a Long Beach, California Veterinarian filed a class action lawsuit against Yelp, claiming extortion. Allegedly, Yelp offered to hide bad review if he purchased paid advertising. When he declined, negative reviews started appearing on his page, some of which were expired and had been reposted under another name.

Although Yelp denied any wrongdoing, it has changed its policy in order to reflect fair review policies. Many Veterinarians have noticed that their positive reviews, which had been previously removed, are now reappearing on their Yelp page.

Has Yelp lost credibility in the Veterinary community? Even if you don't like Yelps review policies, it is impossible to ignore the fact that the site has an estimated 16.5 million users. It makes sense that even if you choose not to be highly active on Yelp then you should at least spend some time reading your reviews and responding to them. It can have a tremendous impact on your reputation.

The Other Guys
There are numerous other social networking sites that you can pursue in order to promote your practice. Social network marketing can occur anywhere where people are talking online. It is an extension of word of mouth advertising, except that you have more control over your image and audience.

Alexa.com can provide you with the rankings of websites. It is probably most beneficial to choose sites that are in the top 50. This way you are able to maximize your marketing efforts and hit as large of a target audience as possible.

Have a Plan
Just like any other part of your marketing plan, social media marketing should be an organized and purposeful effort.

1. Define your goals. Know exactly what you are trying to accomplish and establish milestones. Whether you are using social media strictly for reputation management, or if you are actively trying to sell a service, you should set an attainable goal.

2. Establish clear guidelines. Set rules for who is allowed to post and when. What will the approval process be for content? Who is responsible for monitoring it? Put your guidelines in writing and make sure that the entire staff knows the rules.
3. Develop growth strategies. Identify new techniques and strategies for expanding your involvement and increasing both popularity and your website traffic.
4. Set a defined schedule for how often you will publish content and on what topics. This could be on a monthly or weekly basis.

Example Schedule for Small Animal Practice

- You should plan for content creation and staff training on any promotions one month before you will execute them

Month	What	Who	When	Where
January	Arthritis articles; arthritis screening promotion	Technicians write content and publish	Publish weekly in January	Facebook; Blogs
February	Dental Disease	Veterinarian to write content and publish	Publish weekly in February	Twitter; Facebook
March	Senior Wellness protocol; Senior screening promotion	Technicians write content and publish	Publish weekly in March	Facebook; Blogs
April	Spay/ neuter articles/blogs	Veterinarian to write content and publish	Publish weekly in April	Twitter; Facebook
May	Internal parasites and fecal exams articles	Technicians write content and publish	Publish weekly in May	Facebook; Blogs

Tips for being effective

- Be authentic and contribute content that is valuable to pet owners. Useful tips, how to articles, and educational health alerts are an excellent way to do this. Never just tell a client that they need a service. Instead, educate them as to the need and explain how it will benefit their pet and themselves. Be sure to state things in a language that pet owners can understand. Unless you have a staff member assisting with your site, remember that people may not understand technical terms and medical conditions. Explain things thoroughly in a way that anyone can comprehend.

- Before joining in active conversations, spend some time "lurking". Make sure that you understand what is going on and what is being said. This way you can be sure that you are contributing valuable information to the conversation.

- Be responsive to requests, questions, and other contributions. Social media marketing does not take a lot of specialized training, but you have to be willing to put the time into developing the relationships with people. It is a commitment. If you choose to get involved, you should stay involved.

Conclusion

The world of Social Media works because it allows you to promote your practice to a large group of people, and it is FREE. Sites such as Facebook and Twitter have millions of fans. Although it may be difficult to believe, many companies have used this medium to boost their popularity. Dell Computers, Verizon, and Wal-Mart are just a few of the business giants who tap into the online frenzy.

In summary, social media marketing provides you with a powerful platform with which you can sell a larger volume of higher quality Veterinary service to both your existing clients and find new clients in the process. By influencing groups of pet owners, you are doing something good for your practice, and helping pets achieve better quality medical care at the same time.

Chapter 5
Video Marketing:
Using the Power of Online Video for Your Local Veterinary Practice

Video is growing at an incredible rate on the Internet. With so many video sharing sites these days, you're missing out on a valuable marketing tool for your vet practice if you're not creating content with a camcorder or screen-cast program. However, there's a right way and a wrong way to advertise with video. The worst possible way for your video to come across is as an advertisement. With so many videos out there, you have to really stand out by giving people a reason to watch your clip.

You've got to give them something interesting. If they sense that you're just trying to sell them something, they'll just click away, but if you're providing weekly "how-to" tips, then you're on the right track. As a veterinarian, you should offer weekly video tips for pet owners.

Getting Started with YouTube
Setting up your own YouTube channel is relatively easy. You'll want to register if you don't have an account already. It takes only a few minutes. Make sure that you choose a username that brands your name to your business; a name that people will remember.

For example, wine expert Gary Vaynerchuck of Wine TV has his own YouTube show and his username is WineLibraryTV, the same as his own Web site. Once your account is set up, it's very easy to start posting video; just click "upload video." For each video you upload, you can write a brief description and also include tags. Tags are needed so that people can find your site. So you'll need to put keywords that describe the content of your video.

Customizing your own channel is pretty straightforward, too. Just click on "channel design" and you can set up your own color schemes, fonts, and background images. Now you're ready to start adding content. Beside each new video you create is a URL link that you can use to send people directly to your video, or you can copy the embed code just below that and add it to your own webpage or blog.

Use the embed code feature to paste the code on a lot of my own Web sites. Recently, YouTube has added new features that allow you to cutomize the border and choose from different video sizes.

Getting Subscribers

Just like a blog or a newsletter, you want people to sign up for all of your video updates. This is just another way to gain permission. Once people subscribe to your video channel, you've got a potential customer for as long as they continue to stay subscribed. One of the best ways to get subscribers is to begin subscribing to other video channels.

Try to focus on videos that have markets you want to attract. Veterinarians should look for dog trainers or pet grooming services that have a YouTube channel. You also have the option of becoming a friend of someone, who in turn allows you to share videos privately. All the videos that you post will then show up on their channel. This can really boost your traffic. To add someone as a friend, go to their profile page. There is a link entitled "Connect with (username)" that you'll want to click. Then you'll go to the "add as a friend" link.

The Bottom Line Is Promotion

YouTube allows you to promote your video to its massive audience. This is one of the biggest features at your disposal. You get a massive amount of traffic if your video is featured on YouTube's home page. Here's the kicker—there are only twelve slots available on the home page, and YouTube updates its site about twice a day. The likelihood that you'll get picked up at first is slim to none.

Another feature that YouTube has added is similar to Pay-Per Click Advertising. You can decide where you would like your videos to appear and place bids for those category keywords. Just like Google adwords, you can set your daily budget for how much you want to spend on clicks. This is a quick way to get a large volume of traffic to your channel and then direct them to your site.

The most important thing to remember in all of this is to be promoting your primary business Web site.With all of the latest changes that You-Tube has made, it's easier than ever.There is now a feature that allows you to add annotations within your video, so you can put the address of your main Web site within the video as a reminder for people to visit.You can also add a clickable link within the the description box so that others can click straight to your site.

Get Your Video to Spread

There are a number of other video sites you'll want to utilize besides YouTube. A great tool that will help you upload video to all of them at once is called TubeMogel. You can find it at www.tubemogel.com. Just sign up for a free account and you can have your videos sent to You-Tube and other similar sites such as Vimeo, Viddler, Yahoo, Metacafe, and others with just a few clicks. It's a simple way to direct traffic back to your site. If you look at a lot of the top video marketers, they tend to post their videos at every possible sharing site online. If your video is really eye-catching or provocative, there's a chance that your video will be picked up and spread around the web.Your video could end up on Web sites you've never heard of. I suppose that's why they call it viral marketing. Listed below are a few suggestions for getting your video to spread like wildfire:

- Be genuine—don't be a fake. People can see right through it if you have a canned speech. Relax and have fun with it. Some of the best videos are those in which people just shoot with nothing more than a cheap webcam.
- Be entertaining—don't just talk about your practice and what you do; give some real results. Think of a company like Blendtech. They have a website called *WillitBlend.com* where they show videos of their popular blenders chewing up anything you can think of. No sales talk is as effective as seeing that blender chop up an iPhone.
- Give Value—Give people a reason to spend their time watching your show. What about a weekly health and fitness show for pets?

Again you don't have to be fancy when it comes to production. The most popular YouTube video, "Evolution of Dance," was done with a low-budget camera, and it currently has over 115 million views.

The desire to have the perfect video is what keeps many from doing video marketing. Don't worry about being perfect. Just grab a camera and start shooting. To find out the tools we recommend for getting started with online video, visit VetNetMarketing.com.

Chapter 6
Podcast Marketing:
The Value of Creating Audio Content for Your Veterinary Practice

Have you ever thought what it would be like to host your own radio show? Think of all the business you could get just from from being the go-to expert on the radio.You might not make it on the air the traditional way, but you can start your own radio show online and it only takes a few short minutes to get started.

I'm talking about podcasting. Podcasting has been around for the last few years (it has slowed in popularity with the explosion of online video), but there are still a couple of outlets I would recommend for getting traffic and promoting your business. BlogTalkRadio.com and Podomatic.com are two that I want to discuss.

A podcast is simply a series of audio files that can be distributed online through webfeeds.These webfeeds can then send the podcasts to iTunes, allowing listeners to download the audio content onto their portable iPod. Through iTunes, listeners can subscribe to your podcast and these will be automatically downloaded into their iTunes application each time you produce new content.

We host an Internet marketing show on BlogTalkRadio.com. Our show is on for thirty minutes every Saturday morning.We discuss all subjects related to Internet marketing and occasionally conduct an interview with a special guest on the show.You can find the show at www.bibpodcast.com.

Setting up your own show is very simple. First, you sign up for an account and once you are a member you can start scheduling your own show. Since the shows on BlogTalkRadio are live, you have to schedule your show in advance.

You can make your show for as long as you want. The format works just like a real radio show. BlogTalkRadio gives you a guest number so callers can actually call into your show.There is also a chat feature so listeners can instant message questions or comments as well.You can even add bumper music at the beginning for an intro or create a commercial that you play during your show. If you're consistent in hosting these shows, you can build a huge following and maybe even get some big time sponsors.

Once you've done your first show, BlogTalkRadio gives you the html code for a player to post on your blog or Web site so visitors to your site can listen to your show without logging onto BlogTalkRadio's site. Podomatic.com is another Web site I've used for hosting my podcasts.The podcasts on this site are not recorded live.You can actually do the show whenever you want using a digital recorder, which is what I used in the early days of doing podcasts, or you can use a free software program called Audacity, a very simple sound recorder that allows you to edit audio files before you post them online.

Adding "Juice" To Your Online Marketing
Podcasting is one of the best ways to add major search engine juice to your site. For each of the podcast shows that you create, you are allowed to enter keywords into that site. BlogTalkRadio allows you to add five keywords for each new show that you host. For my Internet marketing show, I usually choose keywords related to the topic of my show that are heavily searched for online.

Again, Google loves unique content.The more often you host a show, the more your rankings will climb. Use your podcast to promote your main Web site by talking about it at the end of your show or adding links to your posts. (You can also add blog posts along with your podcast.)

Build a Subscriber List
Much like email marketing, you want to build a following. With podcasting, you have the option of creating a free or paid for program; although it is highly unlikely people will pay to listen to podcasts these days with so much other free information. But the value in podcasting is building a listenership on iTunes or a fanbase on BlogTalkRadio who listen to your show each and every week.

If you do this and provide good audio content, you can attract a large group of buyers who trust what you say. Developing Your Own Theme Show If you're thinking of hosting your own show, use BlogTalkRadio to host your live show and then take the audio file and upload it to your Podomatic account, as well.

The more listeners you have, the better. As I mentioned, you can schedule your show times in advance, so if you are thinking of having a weekly show, make sure you try to stay consistent with the time and day of the week. The more consistency you have, the more live listeners you're likely to gain.

As I mentioned, we host an Internet marketing show every Saturday at 10:30 AM—same time, same channel. You can use your email marketing campaign to send out reminders of your upcoming show each week. Let them know what the topic will be. By doing a weekly show over and over each week, you'll be seen as the go-to veterinarian expert. Dan Miller, author of 48 Days to The Work You Love, has a wonderful podcast each week on finding meaningful work that you love. I have listened to his show for about three years now.

He does his show with nothing more than his computer, a headset, a sound mixer, and the free sound editing program, Audacity. His show has more than 120,000 downloads per month. I love podcasting because it's a simple way to get content out about your area of expertise. And once it's up, it stays up. We still get traffic from shows we've done two or three years ago!

Chapter 7
Referral Marketing:
How to Create a Swarm of Referral Business for Your Veterinary Practice

Most veterinary practice owners have heard that increasing a customer base through referrals is an inexpensive and effective marketing technique. However, many Veterinary hospitals fail to do so in a meaningful and organized way that will generate substantial results. In fact, 42% of Veterinary Practices do not actively encourage referrals from existing clients.

Of the percentage of veterinary hospitals that do actively encourage referrals, the vast majority fail to develop a systematic formula. This trend is very consistent among all types of hospitals, including small animal, specialty, exotic, and referral practices alike. It is not surprising that Veterinarians find limited success... a successful formula entails much more than sending thank you cards.

If you do not have a winning system in place for getting your clients to refer you, then you are missing an easy and cost-effective way to attract new customers. In fact, developing an organized approach will not only work, it will generate tons of high quality clients for your practice.

Why are client referrals so powerful?

The reason that client referrals are such strong medicine is because they come from a highly credible source, outside of the Veterinary organization. People believe in recommendations that come from someone that they know and trust. There is no doubt that the referral is sincere and reliable because the person referring them has no ulterior motive.

This is especially true if your practice is more expensive than others in your area are. This is because it focuses the referral on the quality of medicine that you practice, instead of price.

While there are certainly a number of veterinary hospitals and vaccine clinics that have maintained a thriving business based on selling discount services, they generally attract lower quality clients, who spend less overall on veterinary care for their pets.

You will find that referred clients are less price-sensitive because they have already heard about the quality of your practice. You will find that most prospects that you gain through a referral will accept your recommendations more readily, even if the service is expensive.

Clients that give referrals become more loyal to your Veterinary Practice. They become emotionally invested in your success, and the bond with your practice will become stronger. The Physiological factor behind this is ego. People want to brag to their friends and neighbors about what they perceive as valuable, they want to feel important, or they want their friends and family to share the same experiences as they do.

The best part about referral programs is that it cost the practice almost nothing to implement. What other form of advertising can accomplish so much for so little?

Quality Medicine Does Not Always Equal Many Referrals

It goes without saying that the success of any referral program is dependent on the quality of medicine and service that your Veterinary Practice offers. However, it does not mean that because you offer high quality medicine and service that your clients will automatically refer you.

In fact, it you do not ask for referrals, it may never occur to your clients to provide them. A good way to look at it is to view your "quality medicine and service" as the foundation for your program. Your clients are the raw materials, with which you must design a deliberate prescription for building your referral program.

Developing your referral system may seem like an awkward task, but the good news is that your clients actually WANT to give you referrals. You just need to show them how.

Word Of Mouth Advertising and Referral-Based Marketing Are Not the Same

When you ask Veterinarians how they get referrals, they will often reply that they get their referrals from word-of-mouth advertising. Although these two things are completely different, most people do not realize it.
Word of mouth advertising is a casual recommendation that is made during the course of a conversation.

There is no forethought or panning, and it will be generally based on the client's perception of their experience at your practice. You control over word of mouth advertising is limited to providing the client with a positive interaction at every patient visit. While this is an important form of advertising, it differs greatly from referral-based marketing.

Referral-based marketing is a process that you methodically plan and implement, with the intention of producing predictable results. Your clients provide you with the names of potential clients, which in marketing terminology are referred to as "leads".

The Veterinary hospital will follow up on these leads by sending them targeted advertising (sales letter, promotional email, brochures, or phone calls). The ultimate goal is to "convert" the referral into a high quality client.
Did a light bulb just turn on? It should have. In Veterinary medicine, we have a tendency to blunder around referral marketing without ever understanding what it is or how powerful it can be.

The potential for creating additional revenue through referrals can be astounding. If, for example, you were able to attract twenty two referral clients a month, and they each spent an average of $200 during one visit, then by the end of the year you would have generated an extra $52,000 of revenue for your practice.

So, how many referral leads do you have to pursue to gain those extra twenty-two clients? The answer to this question is a little more complicated. It really depends on how effective your marketing materials and techniques are at turning these leads into office visits. Marketers refer to this as a "conversion rate". On a very basic level, a reasonable goal is to aim for a 50% conversion rate. Therefore, if you want to attract 22 new clients a month, you should collect a minimum of 44 referrals.

How to Ask for Referrals
If you accept the fact that Veterinary Hospitals are selling services, and that the ability to sell is an important factor in creating a successful practice, then consider how vital referrals are to professional sales people. Studies have demonstrated that sales people who focus on generating high quality referrals will earn four to five times the industry standard. Imagine how healthy your veterinary practice would be if it could increase its revenue on the same scale.

Now that you understand that generating referrals is not the same thing as asking your clients to say nice things about you, it should become easier to create a clear vision for success.
The single, most important factor to developing a successful system is that you have to change the way that you think about referrals. In reality, you most likely know that referrals will not materialize out of thin air and you have to ask for them.

In a Veterinary Practice, the opportunity to do that presents itself with every member of the staff. From the receptionists, technicians, and Veterinarians, create a detailed plan for who will be responsible for this. You must commit to training yourself and your staff to ask consistently for referrals. Not occasionally, not when everyone feels like it or is having a good day, not when the technician thinks that the client like them, but ask every single time a client comes through your doors.
Are you wondering just how to request that referral? While there are many different ways to ask for a referral, they all have one thing in common: phrasing. The way that a question is phrased can have a tremendous impact on the response.

The $50,000 Question
It should not come as a surprise that if you fail to ask for referrals, then you will never get them. However, asking the wrong way is just as big of a mistake as failing to ask at all.

While the exact phrasing of the request will vary depending on the type of referral, there are a few general rules that can be applied to all referral requests.

- The ability to communicate is the #1 need that must be met in order to be successful. You should not only develop it in yourself, but in all of your staff as well.
- Remember that you must paint a "mental picture" in the client's mind that is identical to the mental picture in your mind
- Keep a positive attitude at all times and recognize that positive referrals are earned, and not given. If you show the client that you unfailingly bend over backwards for them, then you will have a created a loyal client who will WANT to give you tons of referrals.

For every right way to ask for a referral, there are also many wrong ways.

Here is a list of common mistakes. How NOT to ask for a referral:
- **Do not** "Suggest" referrals instead of directly asking for them. Many people are afraid to ask a client for a referral, so they ask timidly. An example would be "Mrs. Ferrell, if you happen to know of anyone with a pet who would benefit from our dental cleanings, I would appreciate it if you let them know". Not only is this ineffective, but the uncertainty is subconsciously communicated to the client.
- **Do not** ask only once. While asking once is better than not asking at all, every client visit should provide an opportunity to collect new referrals.
- **Do not** focus on your needs above the client's needs. This is the wrong way to request a referral: "Ms. Hannah, maybe you could help me out and give me the names and phone numbers of a few pet owners that might be interested in trying our service?" Unfortunately, human beings tend to do things that are in our own best interest. The client really does not care as much about "helping you out", as much as they do about the personal gain that they will receive by doing so. Be sure to give the client a reason to provide you with those referrals.
- **Do not** neglect to tell your client what type of referral you are looking for. As simple as this may seem, many people assume that the client knows what type of prospect you are looking for. You may be standing there thinking, "give me a responsible, caring pet owner like yourself", but if you fail to communicate that then you may end up with the lonely lady down the street who has fifteen cats and ten dogs, and is looking for charity veterinary care.

- **Do not** expect the client to think of referrals by themselves. You have to help the client think of referral prospects. Discover whom the client knows and what activities they are involved in. Framing the referral request around a specific group of people will give the client a narrow frame of reference in which to think.

If a veterinary hospital is promoting a "prevent a litter" month, referrals can be generated immediately on the telephone. Here is an example of a conversation that could lead to a few high quality referrals. "Mrs. Bastin, as part of our effort to reduce the unwanted pet population, we are promoting spay and neuter this month by offering a discount for multiple pets.

You can save 20% on the cost of your pet's surgery if we schedule three spays or neuters at the same time. Do you have any other pets or know of a couple of friend's with a pet that need to be spayed or neutered and that would benefit from the discount? "

If you are promoting a doggie daycare, instead of outright asking for a referral, you might say instead, "Mr. Doolittle, I have found that when a dog starts a different daycare program they can often be timid because everything is new. It may help to have a couple of friends bring their dogs for the first day. This way he can settle into our program with playmates that he is already acquainted with. Of course, there would be no charge to your friends."

As you can see from the examples, by being creative in the way that referrals are requested, you can establish a win-win relationship with your client. They (and their pet) will receive a benefit that can be shared with their friends and family, while creating leads for your practice.

A Word about Customer Service and Opportunity
Regardless of how well you plan, your referral program will never amount to anything if you do not start with great customer service. Many Veterinary Practice owners fail to know what goes on between their staff and their clients. This is a monumental mistake, because the client is subconsciously judging your quality of medicine by the sum of their experience at your practice.

A negative interaction with another member of the veterinary team can quickly change a client's perception from a "job well done" into disappointment with his or her overall visit. This is preventable by instating strict customer service policies that every team member must follow.

With a strong customer service base to stand on, the Veterinary Practice is able to take advantage of a number of opportunities to increase their referral base. A few occasions to build relationships and turn your client into a lifetime customer are:

- The moment a client complains about your service. This may seem strange, but complaints are actually beneficial to the veterinary practice. Although there are clients that you will never be able to please, most unsatisfied customers can be appeased by just knowing that you are listening to what they are saying and care that they are unhappy (even if they are wrong). This is an excellent opportunity to not only identify weak areas in your practice, but also to show the client how great your customer service is.

- When a new client returns for a second visit. Obviously, the practice has done something well if a client is returning to you. Have the staff engage them in conversation about what they liked about their visit, let them know that they are appreciated, and look for opportunities to increase referrals through them.

The moment a client needs a favor from you. By cultivating your relationship with your regular clients, you are showing them that you genuinely care about their needs (and the needs of their pet).

- Whenever you see your client in public. Take the time to say hello, and ask how the client is doing. This transforms your relationship from being strictly Doctor-Patient to one of a more personal nature.
- If you have made a mistake that has caused the client a hardship. This can be emotional or financial, or simply an inconvenience to the client, but always be honest about mistakes. By owning up to them and then showing the client that you are making great strides to correct them, you will gain respect and loyalty.

The Two Different Types of Referral Programs

When you consider the source for your referral program, you are not limited to just your client base. While your existing clients are certain to be your most enthusiastic referrers, you can also generate leads from other influential people who have never tried your veterinary service.

When developing your system for generating referrals, the primary focus should be on your existing clients' first, and other influential people, or "centers of influence" second.

Centers of Influence and the 80/20 Rule

Your existing clients can testify, first hand, as to your quality care and service, so they should be your best referrers. However, there is a lot of new business that can be garnered through center of influence marketing.

You hear this term quite a bit in other professions, but not so often in Veterinary applications. The basic idea is that instead of chasing prospects one at a time through yellow page or newspaper ads, you are able to use an influential leader to address a group of potential new clients. Are you wondering who, exactly, your "centers of influence are? In the veterinary world, this would comprise any person whose group includes pet owners.

The general rule is that if you spend your time prospecting 20% of the top centers of influence, it will produce 80% of the results. For organizing your referral system, center of Influence marketing is divided into two separate tiers.

Tier One Centers of Influence

Tier 1 centers of influence are the people who provide complimentary services and products. They have a direct connection to the Veterinary industry because they are pet related businesses.
If you choose these people well, there is a lot of potential for creating positive relationships that will pay dividends in the form of new clients. Examples include dog trainers, horse trainers, pet storeowners, feed storeowners, farriers, local dog clubs and adoption groups, cat fancier organizations, groomers, and animal photographers. There are also many specialties in the Veterinary industry that may not compete with your practice directly.

All of these occupations deal with pets, and can be choice picking. Look for the ones that seem to be the busiest and the most successful.
Your goal with these tier one referral opportunities is to be the first person on their minds when someone asks about pet health issues.

With this at the forefront of your thought, sit down and brainstorm with your staff about ways to accomplish this. Because your staff members are frequently pet owners also, they may be able to provide you with additional insight as to identifying and approaching these businesses.

Here are a few ideas that you can use as examples to help you start.

- Return the favor. If you want these people to send you referrals, then you must return the favor. Identify the most successful businesses that offer services or products that match your quality standards, and refer to them with confidence. Make it a team goal to not only refer often, but to refer quality clients.
- Sponsor a networking event, luncheon, or dinner where you invite several of your tier one centers of influence. Do not invite competitors. Discuss marketing techniques and share your ideas.
- Keep them involved with your practice by including them in your newsletter list. If your newsletter does not contain information about the latest innovations and happenings at your practice, it should. This not only keeps your referrers connected, it also keeps your clients in touch with what is going on.
- If there is a guest speaker or marketing seminar going on in your town, invite them to go with you. Make a fantastic, high-class statement by having a limousine pick them up, and serve wine or fine drinks. Things such as this, when done in good form and with impact, improves your image and will make them more eager to refer to you.
- If you are going to make an effort to establish quality tier one referral relationships, then you must commit to making the time to do a good job. Be careful about expanding this network beyond what you have the inclination to maintain. It is far better to have only one or two quality referrers that you nurture, than to have many that are neglected. A haphazard approach will be ineffectual and a waste of your resources.
- Consider co-hosting a fun public event. You can collect names, addresses, and email contacts through sign-up sheets or raffles. The more unique and fun these events are, the higher the opportunity is for generating leads. Here are a few examples, but you are only limited by a lack of imagination.
- Hold a contest for the pet and owner that look the most alike
- Hold a pet beauty contest, and let the audience vote for the cutest, ugliest, or most talented, pet.
- Host an dog training, cat training, or first aid educational seminar

Tier Two Centers of Influence

Tier two centers of influence are the people whom you know that are not in a pet related business, but that you meet with on a regular basis. They can also multiply your marketing efforts. These people may include some of the following:

- Friends
- Neighbors
- Fellow hobbyists
- Clergy
- Lawyers
- Accountants
- Financial planners
- Equipment repair people
- Pest control
- Dentist, chiropractor, or doctor's office

Any person or place that you routinely do business with can also be included on this list. If you always fill up at the same gas station, shop at the same grocery store, eat at the same restaurant, or buy coffee every day from the same café, then you should include them on your list.

These business owners may have no idea what it is that you actually do for a living, so make an opportunity to invite them to lunch and discuss it. Share stories about customer experiences in your practice, and talk about developing a referral system.

If you wanted to pursue this idea even further, you could host a dinner or mixer for a group of these businesses. Learn more about them, what it is that they do, and whom they may know. Putting forth the effort to nurture these relationships can be very profitable for both sides.

The Power of Cross Promotions

Cross promoting is an easy, powerful, and creative way to out-market large veterinary chains that have a much heftier budget than you might have. The idea behind cross-promotional marketing is that you are collaborating with a high quality complimentary business to share each other's client list and marketing resources.

It allows you to join forces with another highly credible business that shares your target audience, your tier one centers of influence. Marketing efforts may be conventional techniques, such as "bundled" offerings and co-hosting events. It can also entail unconventional cause-related marketing.

- Print joint promotional messages on each other's receipts
- Drop each other's brochures into checkout bags
- Share local advertising opportunities and split the cost
- Give clients a free (or discounted) product or service from a participating partner whenever they buy something that month from all of the partners listed in an ad or on a promotional item.

As a very basic example, if you are an equine practitioner, you may choose to collaborate with a local horse training facility. Your promotion could require the client to purchase a month of prepaid training service, and a full equine examination, vaccinations, and a fecal test. The reward for the client purchasing all of these things could be a discount on the second month's training and a free deworming.

Ten Questions That Can Help You Become a Networking Pro
Many people in the Veterinary industry do not like to network. Between running your business, practicing medicine, and keeping current of the latest medical trends, who has time for establishing a network? Besides, Veterinary Medicine is about the animals and not the people... right?
Unfortunately, to be a successful Veterinary business owner, you cannot afford to bury your nose into patients and textbooks. If you are going to put these marketing techniques into action, you have to network with other people.

Here are ten simple questions that you can use to break the ice when networking with other business owners. These questions serve to open the conversation, create good feelings, and allow them to share their expertise with you. People like to talk about themselves, so it is an easy starting point.

1. How did you come to own a _____ (grooming, training, etc.) business?
2. What do you like the most about _____ (being a farrier, photographer, chiropractor, etc.)?
3. What do you do that makes you different from your competition?
4. What advice would you give someone who wanted to go into the same business?
5. What is the one thing that you would do with your business if you knew that you could not fail?
6. What significant changes are occurring in your industry?
7. What do you think the future trends are in your industry?

8. What are your favorite marketing techniques for your business?
9. What type of strange things do you see in your line of work?
10. How would you like people to describe your service (or product)?

Obviously, your conversation with these people should not feel like an interview, so you would not ask every question on the list. The goal is to choose the ones that are the most appropriate and that you feel comfortable using. It will also help you gather valuable information with which you can use to identify further referral opportunities.

Start a Referral Group
You are not alone in your desire to gain more referral business! Referral groups are a great way to create a support network of businesses that help each other. These people do not necessarily have to come from other pet related industry, they can simply be other business people that you know or admire.

The benefit to developing this type of personal network is that is provides a support system for all of your marketing efforts. You should meet with your group on a regular basis to discuss marketing ideas, evaluate what you have tried and what works, and look for new opportunities to try something new.

Find ways to contribute to your group so that people can see a real benefit from it. Education and promotion are two areas that everyone can use to grow their businesses. By discovering new ways to do this, you will be well on your way to increased revenue.

Tapping Into Your Most Valuable Asset: Your Existing Client Base
When it comes to evaluating the value of your Veterinary Practice, you know how much your physical assets are worth. However, what about the value of your client list? If you wanted to sell it, it would not be worth much to another Veterinarian. Nevertheless, it is priceless to the health of your practice.

You are probably very familiar with the concept that every client has a "lifetime value". This is the amount of revenue that a pet owner will generate for your practice, throughout the lifetime of their relationship with you.
For this reason, it is important to ensure that your customer database is kept up to date and accurate.

Files should be randomly audited for information such as current address, phone numbers, and email contacts. Have your front desk staff update them as part of the check in process at every visit. If a client address has not been updated in the last three years, then there is likelihood that your marketing dollars will be wasted.

Know who your best clients are. This goes back to the old 80/20 rule. The top 20% of your clients will provide you with 80% of your revenue. Focus your referral efforts heavily on this group of people. They are not only your top spenders, but they are also the most loyal customers.

The top 20% of your clients may vary from year to year. How do you stay on top of whom these people are? Your veterinary management software should offer you a report function that will tell you not only who they are, but also on which services they spend their money. Once you have identified them, your software will allow you to assign a class code, or rating to their account. This way, any team member who pulls them up in your system will be alerted to whom they are.

Conclusion
Establishing a referral system with your customers and other influential people is how many businesses grow from average to outstanding. By making use of all of the possibilities for generating referrals, you will be light years ahead of your competition. You certainly do not have to be a marketing guru. You only have to be willing to put forth the effort and then sit back and enjoy the money making machine that you have created.

The Referral Marketing Plan
Step 1: Identify WHO will be your referrers

1. Top 20% of your existing client base
2. The rest of your clientele
3. Tier 1 centers of influence
4. Tier 2 centers of influence

Step 2: Create a promotion for each category of referrers
- Create your promotion or event. Your promotion should describe the "reward" that you will provide them with if they give you a specific number of referrals. Change the promotion or event up on a monthly basis, so that you can offer them new rewards, and continue collecting referral information.

- Create the reward. Make sure the reward is tangible and something that they will see the benefit in right away. You do not want to make them wait six months before they can redeem their reward. This will keep them referring to you.
- Plan for who will be responsible for implementing and carrying out the details of the promotion. Hold a staff meeting, or create detailed memos so that all of your team members are on board.

Step 3: Advertise your Promotion

Create a method for promoting your promotion. In the case of using your centers of influence, you will most likely be dealing with them directly, but you still need a plan for how you are going to approach these people.

- Use your website to spread the word. A simple ad on your home-page is enough to get people's attention. If you want to include more details, then consider adding a header and listing your promotion under it.
- Print flyers to staple to every client receipt.
- Have the front desk staff routinely ask the new clients "Have you heard about our such and such promotion?"

- Post "ad boards" in your reception areas.
- Include it in your newsletter.

Step 4: Track your referrals carefully

Keep up with who your most active referrers are. This way you can offer a special reward for the top few. This not only shows your appreciation, but also motivates them to keep up the good work.

- Keep a notebook at the reception desk for staff to log the names of referrers.
- Have the reception staff ask every client "Is there someone whom we can thank for referring you to us?"
- Check to see if your management software has a feature for inputting referral information. Many of them do.

Step 5: Reward, Reward, Reward

You already know that you have to reward your referrers, but do not forget about showing your appreciation by sending thank you cards. It is important to thank everyone who refers to you, regardless of whether it came from word of mouth advertising or a direct referral that you so-licited.

Step 6: Rinse and Repeat
Keep your referral effort fresh. Change them frequently and brainstorm ideas that are both creative and fun. Once you have a plan it place, it will become an integrated part of your practice.

Chapter 8
Hot Off the Press:
How to Make Free Publicity Work for Your Veterinary Practice

Hollywood celebrities know that they can make their careers shine through the power of publicity. What does this fact have to do with Veterinary medicine? Regardless of how long your veterinary practice has been established, publicity marketing is a powerful, free tool that you can use to drive new business through your front door. The media can play a crucial role in developing and managing a practice's reputation.

Pet owners want Veterinarians that are empathetic and have a passion for animals. The price that you charge for services is irrelevant, as long as the client believes that your recommendations are in their pet's best interest, primarily. Publicity marketing is an easy and effective method for spreading that message.

Publicity works. The secret behind this is that people tend to believe what they read in print. Mass media lends an air of credibility without the client ever setting foot inside of your practice. If your marketing is done well, with forethought and a little planning, you can catapult the public's interest in your practice, without spending a dime in advertising.

You ain't in Kansas anymore, Dorothy!
Media marketing is not just for Hollywood celebrities! The Veterinary industry is evolving and there has been a noticeable shift in other business away from traditional advertising, towards the world of free publicity. Why? Publicity generates as many, or more, consumer impressions as paid advertising. These impressions can translate into phone calls, client visits, and new business.

The glitz and glamour of Hollywood aside (and even if you are in Kansas) publicity marketing will work for you. The following report contains simple steps that you can implement for getting free publicity for your Veterinary Practice.

Although you may not use all of the concepts discussed, they will give you a base from which you can develop your own, individual ideas. By taking advantage of the powerful social and cultural influence that mass media has on an audience, you can put yourself miles ahead of your competition!

Step 1: Developing Your "Message Points"
"Compassionate and Competent Care... It's not just out motto, it's what we do everyday"

Your business message points are four of five reasons that people should choose you for pet care over other veterinarians. It is likely that if you have developed a marketing message for your practice, you already know your message points.

They should be the highlight of why your business is attention-worthy and unique. When developing these points, do not focus on trying to "sell" your service, instead concentrate on the things that you are passionate about in your profession. Here are a few tips for developing key message points.

- Explain who you are and what you do
- Make a list of unique features about your practice

Examples:
- We are the only hospital in our area that offers in-clinic chemotherapy, as cancer is a leading killer of beloved pets
- We have invested heavily in our state of the art patient monitoring equipment, in order to ensure a safe anesthetic experience.
- We are happy to provide our patients with visiting radiologist on Tuesdays, and a board certified surgeon on Mondays and Fridays
- We know how important it is to offer extended hours to accommodate working families, so we do not close until 8 P.M.

The purpose of defining these message points is so that you have a well-focused message that can be communicated in a very short period. Whether you are at a gathering of business owners, participating in an interview, or writing a press release, these key points about your practice will provide you with an outline to ensure that the right message is being communed. In order to be effective, these points should be the primary theme, and they should be delivered consistently.

Step 2: Develop Your Media Kit

A Summary of Brand "YOU"

All Veterinary Practices should have some type of basic media kit. A public relations agency can develop one for you, or you can create your own. If you choose to make your own, be certain that you are able to create professional, classy material. Nothing says "desperate amateur" louder that a poorly developed media kit. Take the time to investigate high quality folders that are branded, or unique and crafty alternatives to cheap paper folders. Remember, people are judging you based on the appearance of your folder.

Your media kit should contain the following:

- A press release
- A photograph of you, your facility, and your staff
- The practices biography, highlighting special accomplishments, such as AAHA certification
- A testimonial page full of quotes and praises
- Your business card
- A detailed service brochure

Keep the materials brief and to the point. If a person is not able to determine, with speed and ease, what your practice is about, then your folder may end up in the trash. If it is also too cluttered or disorganized, or full of annoying confetti, it may share the same fate.

That Is Great. So What Is It For?

Your media kit is presented whenever ANYONE asks for more information about your practice. This request may be in response to an interview (for newspaper, magazine, radio, or television) request, or a follow up on a press release.

Do not make the mistake of simply mailing your media kit out to every journalist that you can find contact information for. Reserve your media kit for those that are actually interested, or as a follow up to press releases that you have submitted. It is also a fantastic tool to hand out whenever you host an event or speak in public.

Step 3: Write a Press Release

A press release, news release, or media release is a written communication aimed at members of the media, to announce a newsworthy event. It is intended to provide reporters and editors with the basic information needed for them to develop a story. They are typically e-mailed, faxed or mailed to assignment editors at newspapers, magazines, radio stations and television networks.

This is a common technique used by public relation firms to generate favorable attention for their client's products, services, or events. The sheer volume of press releases that they receive everyday overwhelms assignment editors. In order for yours to be read and considered for a story or interview, it must catch the attention of the editor. Short, punchy, and compelling stories are given the most consideration, so it helps to have a few creative writing skills.

Press releases must follow a specific format. Poor quality press releases incorrectly formatted or with basic spelling mistakes, can actually hurt your efforts because you will be seen as sloppy and unprofessional. For help in formatting a dynamic press release, you can view the article at http://www.publicity123.com

Specialize, Sensationalize and Get Your Story Covered!

In order to up the chances that your press release will be noticed, you know that it has to be forceful, creative, correctly formatted, and error free. However, what type of stories receive coverage, and from what type of medium?
Your content should be targeted towards a specific medium. Newspapers and magazines generally want interesting pieces that their readers will find value in reading. Educational and informative content are ideal.

Radio stations tend to like quirkier content, anything that is weird, funny, or controversial. Think about what you commonly hear on radio programs and brainstorm stories that fit with their character. Television gravitates towards stories that provide them with great visual imaging.

All mediums love heart-warming human-interest stories. The very nature of the human / companion animal bond provides loads of material for a tear jerking story. If you can think of a recent case that touched you or amazed you, then you have all of the ingredients for generating a lot of free publicity.

Tips from Public Relation Professionals

Professional public relations people know the trade secrets for submitting press releases and obtaining favorable results. Review these tips carefully, as they can prevent you from making costly errors when presenting your idea to the media.

- Assign a code number to all of your press releases. This enables you to track the results.

- Put your contact information in the middle of the press release. This reduces the possibility that your information will be edited or cut out of the top or bottom.

- Be sure that you use an "angle" to turn common news into spectacular content.

- Read a lot of newspapers and magazines to learn how a journalist writes.

- Writing dynamic headlines is the number one need for great press releases. Look at the National Enquirer, Cosmopolitan, or Reader's Digest and copy the same headline style.

- Keep it short and sweet. One page, 250 words, double spaced is ideal

- Tell your story, as you would like to see it in print.

The Eight Deadly Sins
Of course, for everything that you are doing right, there are lists of things that can be done wrong.

Avoid any potential pitfalls by double-checking your work for any of these eight deadly sins.

1. Providing inaccurate information, especially contact information. Press releases must be accurate, complete, and specific.

2. Sending them in too late. Press releases should be submitted at least two weeks before a scheduled event.

3. Failing to provide real "news" value. A newsworthy event is one that is unique and different. If it isn't unique, then it isn't news.

4. Blatantly promoting your practice is not acceptable in a press release. Avoid over commercializing by using words such as "spectacular", or "one-of-a- kind"

5. Failing to include contact information. If you want your story covered, you need to be sure to tell them who to get ahold of.

6. NEVER call them to see if they received your press release. Statements such as "I was just calling to see if you got my press release" will brand you as a pest and unprofessional. Most editors and reporters do not have the time to follow up on this for you.

7. Using outdated contact references. Take the time to double check that the person you are sending the release to still works there and that their address has not changed.

Twelve Ways to Make Your Veterinary Practice Newsworthy

Remember, the media publishes news. In order for you to take advantage of publicity marketing, you must be newsworthy. The media's purpose is not to provide you with free advertising, so your content must be compelling and useful. Here are a few ideas, outside of the human-interest angle, that you can consider for generating notable content.

- Hold a fun event. Consider hosting a themed pet costume contest. Hire a celebrity judge, have him bring his/her dog, and invite local television stations to cover the event.

- Do a customer survey, and include fun and unusual questions. For example, ask how them if their dog wears a specific type of clothing, how often they tell their cat that they love them, or whether or no they would choose their pet over their spouse. Write articles about the results, and do not forget to post them in your lobby for all of your clients to see.

- Develop an annual award that you give out to someone in the community or another pet related business. For example, you could create an award for the business that has done the most to benefit the welfare of feral cats in your neighborhood.

- Offer surprising and astonishing pet or veterinary facts. Companies, such as Merial and Hills, use this technique to promote their products. Think about the statement, "Dental disease affects up to 80% of pets over the age of three, and just like humans, there can be serious consequences of poor dental health."

- Use current events to create a newsworthy topic. For example, when the recession was the main topic, an article about how it affected animal welfare in your area.

- Be the first veterinarian to do *anything*. The first veterinarian to give your employees ownership in your business, the first one to offer free grooming with every surgery, or the first one to offer laser surgery for every patient.

- Sponsor a local community service project. You could offer to provide free vaccinations on site at a local pet adoption drive or advertise homeless pets on your website

- Hold a dog / owner look-alike contest. Hire a celebrity judges and invite local media to cover the event. You could even invite reporters to participate, and create an individual class for the pet owning media.

- Host a one-of-a -kind themed customer appreciation event, such as "Arabian Nights", complete with belly dancers, and authentic music and food, or a magical theme party in which your clients can bring their pets and children to watch magicians do tricks.

- Close down your practice for one day and have your staff donate their time at a local pet rescue or shelter. Imagine the press that you would receive for that one!

- Be a mentor. Invite students or Boy Scout explorer groups into your veterinary practice for demonstrations, and talk to them about what it means to be a veterinarian.

As you can see, ideas for making your veterinary practice newsworthy can ingenious and creative. The possibilities are unlimited, and your staff may enjoy helping you come up with possibilities that are both fun and practical.

A few ideas that other business have used are:
- A pest control company in Texas holds a "biggest roach" contest every summer. He has established tremendous notoriety and credibility in Texas, as well as making national news!

- A company that markets odor control products hosts a "stinkiest sneakers" contest

- A limousine company in Indiana decided to help children in need of transportation to medical care facilities, and at the same time have fun with an event to raise awareness for a cause. They collaborated with a local radio station to host a "who has the biggest limo" contest.

A Word on Public Speaking

Establishing yourself as an expert in the field of Veterinary Medicine is as easy as just getting your name out there. Offer to speak to local rescue groups, schedule pet care workshops, and offer to visit schools. Make a point to appear at chamber of commerce functions, and add your name to their speakers list.

Take along plenty of business cards to hand out at these events. If you feel that you lack the social skills needed to be a dynamic public speaker, classes are usually offered, or ask a friend for some honest advice. Here are a few things to keep in mind when making a public presentation:

- Know the name of the hosts and use them when responding to questions. This dramatically connects you to the host and shows the audience that you are attentive. Make a point to have a conversation with them before your speech.

- Know the format of the event in advance and how much time that you have been allotted. You want to make sure that you address all of the key points about yourself, and your practice. Knowing the length of your speech will help you determine how quickly you need to communicate these points and how much time you can spend on them.

- Never make up our speech on the spot just because you are the expert. Plan to deliver at least three of your key message points and include content that people will receive value from listening to.

- Watch out for "Ted Turner" disease! Avoid using "ers" and "ahs", and "ums" in your speech. The audience may tune you out and it can make you appear uneducated and insecure. Practicing your speech often will help you avoid this pitfall.

- Be careful of using a lot of technical jargon. Remember that your audience is the general public, and that they do not have a Veterinary degree. They most likely will not know a duodenum from an ileus, so explain things in a language people can understand.

- Bring visual aids with you to demonstrate what you are talking about. Props, graphics, and images help the audience relate to what you are saying.

- Send a thank you note. This can help you be invited to speak at another event. You can email a thank you note, or send one the old-fashioned way, just so long as you send one. People want to know that you enjoyed speaking at the event and that you would want to do it again.

Position Yourself as a Media Source

If you are persistent, and you do things the right way, you can become the first stop for the media whenever pet related information is needed.

This can happen only after you have established a relationship with the media through he steps outlined above. Once you have proved yourself reliable and knowledgeable, you are in a position to contribute your veterinary expertise to the public.

A few key elements for establishing yourself as a source are:
- Stay on top of the latest trends in Veterinary Medicine
- Build a relationship with members of the media
- Be available on short notice if they call on you
- Prove to them that you can be trusted and that you will deliver
- Inform the media of your expertise and that you are available for them to use as a source
- Watch the news and whenever a Veterinary related topic comes up, call them and remind them that you are available to comment on the story

Write Your Way to Success

"And by the way, everything in life is writable about if you have the outgoing guts to do it, and the imagination to improvise. The worst enemy to creativity is self-doubt." ~Sylvia Plath

Writing columns or education pieces on pet health care is a great way to get your name and your practice noticed. How many times have you read pet health articles in a publication, and thought to yourself, "I could write that"? Well, the good news is that you can, you only have to do it. Take photographs of interesting cases that come through your practice, and then write about it.

Newspapers and magazines often publish informative pieces, as long as the topic is interesting and relevant. There are also several online sources for publishing your content, and you have the double bonus of increasing traffic to your website by submitting to them. It costs you nothing but your time, and you will gain invaluable exposure in return for your efforts.

Online article directories:

www.associatedcontent.com
www.ezine.com

www.squidoo.com
www.suite101.com
www.buzzle.com

Conclusion

Wherever your Veterinary Practice is in its advertising timeline, publicity marketing is a viable and valuable weapon to have in your arsenal. Businesses that take advantage of this system, and do it successfully, find that they grow and thrive, despite the economy. Media attention is usually a positive thing.

When it is handled properly, it can bring in new clients that are already convinced that you are the right Veterinarian for them! Put these valuable techniques to work for you and start generating a buzz about your practice!

References for Submitting Press Releases

Automated Press Releases — Reasonable prices for industry-specific e-mail distribution of releases. www.automatedpr.com/

BookFlash — Just $145 for distribution of news about your book to 5,000+ editors, reviewers, booksellers, librarians, etc. www.bookflash.com/

Business Wire — Efficient vehicle for distributing business-oriented news releases. www.businesswire.com/

Canada NewsWire — Use this distribution service for news specific to Canada. www.newswire.ca/

eReleases — Service that delivers your releases to general and targeted media contacts by email. www.ereleases.com/

Hispanica e-PR — Gets your news out to media in Latin America, Spain and the U.S. www.hispanicapress.com/

HispanicPRWire — If you need to reach Hispanic media in the U.S., use this service. www.hispanicprwire.com/

iMediafax — Service that faxes topical news releases to editors and producers nationwide for $.25 a page. www.imediafax.com/

Internet News Bureau — Email news release distribution service for Web-related material. www.internetnewsbureau.com/

Chapter 9
Direct Mail Marketing

The Secret of Direct Mail Success for Veterinarians

Many veterinarians hear the word "direct mail marketing" and roll their eyes. They think, "I have been there and done that, direct mail marketing doesn't work!" If that statement describes you, then you need to keep reading. There are many reasons why direct mail marketing is still a viable and effective method for attracting new clients to your practice.

Think about the amount of advertisements that you receive in the mail every day. Some of them you read, and some of them you don't. However, that is not the point. We will discuss that in more detail later on. The point is that if direct mail marketing did not produce results, so many companies would not still be using it.

○ Direct mail is like the energizer bunny... it keeps on going, and going, and going. As long as the mail is delivered, then your marketing message will be too. It is a powerful way to deliver your sales pitch to thousands of pet owners, all without you being present or having to say a word.

○ Direct mail works quickly. The turnaround for response time is within one or two weeks. In this time, you will have heard from the majority of the people who are going to respond. This makes it very easy to know whether your campaign was successful, and to track the results.

○ Direct mail allows you to get undivided attention. Unlike other forms of media; a piece of direct mail gives you the best opportunity to focus the recipient's attention on what you have to say. This is because people when people open their mail, they usually give it their undivided attention, as opposed to trying to concentrate on two or three things at once.

Chances are your direct mail campaign was less than satisfying because you really had no idea of what works and what doesn't work. This report will focus on showing you not only how to do direct mail the right way, but also how to decide if a direct mail campaign is right for your practice.

Is it junk mail or the solution they have been looking for?

The argument against direct mail is, of course, that your mail piece will be thrown in the trash before it is even opened. It is "junk mail", a total waste of money. You are bombarding people with things that they don't have the time or desire to read.

This is simply untrue, and for one very important reason: one person's trash is another person's treasure. Junk mail is only junk if the recipient has no interest in the offer that you are sending them. An advertisement that is sent to the wrong list of people is destined for the trashcan.

Think about your own hobbies and interests. Whatever you are "into", or passionate about, is what you are likely to pay attention to. For example, if your passion is bicycling then you are likely to read an advertisement about a new bicycle shop near you. You may even keep the ad for future reference.
The same is true for direct mail marketing of veterinary practices. Unless your advertisement is targeted to people who are crazy about pets, it probably will be thrown away. This is why you must begin any direct mail campaign by identifying the right list of people.

The Mailing List
The number one reason that direct mail campaigns fail are due to the mailing list. If every other element of your campaign is fantastic, but you mail it to people who could care less about veterinary services, then your promotion will flop.

So, how do you identify what types of people should be on your list?
- People who have recently purchased anything pet related
- People within annual income range that indicates that they can afford your service
- People within a specific geographical area
- People that have group associations related to pets: Pet fancier clubs are a great place to look. They are species specific, and sometimes even breed specific.

Is it better to spend money on a direct mail campaign that targets people who MIGHT be interested in veterinary service, or one that you KNOW will be interested in it? Which one do you think would be more successful?

Targeting the right audience is crucial to producing results. If you want to spend your marketing dollars wisely on a direct mail campaign that will work, you must invest in a mailing list that can deliver results.

Mailing List Resources for Veterinarians

A list broker is someone who helps you find the right audience for your veterinary practice. Usually, they earn a percentage on whatever the mailing list costs you. Remember, whatever you spend on obtaining the right list is counter-balanced by the response you receive from your e forts. Therefore, a good list broker will not only save you money in the end, but also help you make money by ensuring that your target market is as narrowly defined as possible.

Allmedia, Inc.
http://www.allmediainc.com
(469) 467-9100 or brokerage@allmediainc.com

Leon Henry, Inc.
http://www.leonhenryinc.com
914-285-3456 or lh@leonhenryinc.com

My Mailhouse Direct
866.588.0499 or mailto:info@mymhd.com
http://www.mymailhousedirect.com/specialty-lists/pet-owner-lists.html

Beach List Direct
(615) 356-1100 Ext. 6305 or mailto:rbeach@beachlistdirect.com
http://www.beachlistdirect.com/Datacards/all-about-dogs-and-cats-mailing-list.asp

1000 Lists
http://www.1000lists.com
469-467-9138 or http://www.1000lists.com/contact-us.html

The Numbers Game

As a veterinarian, you use math every day to formulate successful treatment plans for your patients. Calculating the health of a direct mail marketing campaign is no different. There is some basic terminology that you need to know before you proceed.

- Breakeven point is the amount of service or product that you must sell in order to equal the amount of money you invested in the mailing. (Breakeven point = overhead cost/selling price- product cost)
- Response rate is the number of responses that you receive, divided by the number of mail pieces that were sent. (Response rate = responses/mailings)
- Conversion rate is the number of pet owners that purchased your service or became new clients because of the mailing. (Conversion rate = new clients/ total mailings)

Any campaign should begin with a solid understanding of what your breakeven point is. In order to know whether the breakeven point justifies the expense of a campaign, you have to have a conversion rate estimate. A good conversion rate is about 1%.

As you are calculating, it is important to keep in mind the projected lifetime value of a client. Your goal is to attract new clients, but these clients are going to be repeat customers, ones that return to you year after year or their pet health care needs.

However, the bottom line on any marketing decision is the return on investment. After all, you are in business to make money, altruistic motives aside. Don't get so carried away with planning strategy and technique that you forget about this.

Direct Mail Strategy

Your goal in planning a strategy in a direct mail campaign is to produce mailings that are low risk and highly responsive. This statement exemplifies the basis of what we were talking about earlier. You want to minimize the risk that your advertisement will be discarded and your dollars wasted, while maximizing the potential for the number of new clients you can attract.

Here are some strategies that you can consider that will help you meet those goals.

1. A Radial Direct Mail Campaign

The idea behind radial direct mail campaigns is to send your mailing to pet owners that live in close proximity to your "A" list clients. Often, the format will be a letter that is an endorsement from one of your clients.

"Dear Neighbor,
We just wanted to share some exciting news about Donna Chilton, your Wuthering Heights neighbor on Beavercreek Lane, and her dog "Snooky"! "Snooky" was the September winner of our "cutest pet contest.
With great prizes such a months' worth of premium flea and tick product, a free membership card that entitles her to great discounts on extra services, and a feature photograph in our newsletter, maybe you and your adorable dog could be our next winner?"

2. An Endorsed Joint Venture Mailing

An endorsed venture mailing is a simple concept. Identify a complementary business that you do not compete with, but offers a product or service that would share your client base. You then send them an endorsed letter. For example, if you are a small animal practice, you could send your clients a letter endorsing the local grooming salon. In exchange, the grooming salon would send their clients a letter endorsing you. This method eliminates the need for a mailing list.

3. A Highly Targeted Mass Mailing

As discussed previously, a highly targeted mailing will have the best chance for success. This is the type of campaign where you need to call in the mailing list broker. If you are a small animal practice, you only want to market to dog and cat owners within 15 miles (or whatever distance, depending on your circumstance), that earn over $25,000 annually.

Sequential Mailing

People have a tendency to buy from services that they trust. This is especially true when it comes to their pets. Because of the intense emotional connection that pet's elicit with their owners, it is often necessary for them to hear your message multiple times before they are willing to trust you enough to try you. This is where sequential mailings can be helpful.

Sequential mailings allow you to establish a relationship with the audience. Since veterinary clients have the potential for a substantial lifetime value, you can afford to do more than one mailing. It may be worth doing ten mailings over 20 weeks if your content is good enough to keep their attention.

Each mailing should be linked to the previous mailing. There are many ways to do this, but the easiest is to mention the previous mailing in the new one. If the service that you are promoting is a relatively lower price one, try to limit the number of sequential mailings to no more than three.

It is important to keep up with the amount of time between mailings. For sequential mailing to work, you have to send them one or two weeks apart. If you forget to send them on schedule, the effect will be lost.

Whenever you go fishing, don't forget the bait!
Anytime you go fishing, you have to have the right bait. Even if you follow all of the above steps perfectly, you still won't succeed if you can't hold your audience's attention. In writing, this is often called a "hook". It is something about the mailer that literally hooks them onto your piece and makes them want to keep reading.

The more creative you are with the content, the more fun it is for both you and the recipient.

Here are some ideas for fun and attention getting direct mailers.
- The tasty and healthy dental treat: Include a free dental treat in a mailer that has a theme on a dental promotion. Your letter could start out by saying something like, "You're probably wondering why we are sending you a free dental treat for your dog. Go ahead, grab it and give it to your dog. Although it is just a simple treat for helping to keep your dog's teeth and gums healthy, there is a hidden message behind it. We want you to know how important good dental health is in your dog, and how if neglected, it could lead to serious life threatening health complications".

- The mini-CD: today you can buy mini-cds that are as big as a business card and can be cut into cute shapes. Load your website onto it and include free special reports on relevant health problems that many pet owners may not be aware exist. Include a tour of your facility and a "meet the staff" section, or record yourself giving an introduction and important health message.

- The free id: A free identification tag that has your practice name and phone number on it will let everyone know that a pet is your patient. These can be purchased in bulk, and customized to your practice color and logo. The engraving can say something like, "My owner takes me to ABC Animal Hospital. If you find me, please call xxx-xxx-xxxx." The engraved tag could accompany a letter about your hospital and relevant information about micro-chipping promotions and lost pet services.

Remember, that people look for tangible things when evaluating a service. You have endless opportunity to create this effect through scents, pet friendly products that are mass-produced, and promotional giveaways. Bone shaped or paw print stationary is another great way to do this.

The possibilities for ideas are endless. If you find that you are running short on imaginative ideas, there is a website that can help you brainstorm. http://www.lumpymail.com is a service that specializes in creating creative and unique promotions to help get your mail noticed.

If at first you don't succeed...
Here is where the quote at the beginning of this report comes in. "The successful man will profit from his mistakes and try again in a different way"-Dale Carnegie. Once you have identified a direct mail campaign that works (or doesn't work), you should test it in small ways to see if you can improve your response rate.

In order to do this, you need to know two things: what to change and how to track your results. In deciding what to change, there are a few key factors to keep in mind. The most urgent one is to make ONE single change with each test. Otherwise, it will just become a confusing mess because you will not know which change resulted in a higher (or lower) response rate.

The order of change, by importance is as follows:

1. Mailing list – make sure you are mailing to people who will be interested in what you have to say... no junk mail
2. Envelope- personalization counts

3. Headline – A compelling "hook"
4. Offer – a great offer is more important than the actual copy
5. Post script – experts say that a post script usually gets read
6. Long versus short copy – get to your point quickly so that a reader doesn't lose interest.

As to tracking your response rate, there are many sophisticated ways to do this. For a busy veterinary practice that is on a budget, the simplest way may be to code your campaigns. Give a code on your offer that clients must use when taking advantage of a direct mail offer.

Then have your front desk staff create a log to record the use of the code, along with the client identification number so that it can be cross-referenced if needed. This will allow you to see how much the client is spending based on the offer that you sent.

Veterinary hospitals are notoriously bad for following up on the results of any marketing campaign, so you will have to be diligent in ensuring this is done. If you utilize a practice manager, this is one area where you can defiantly "pass the buck". Put them in charge of reporting the results of each marketing campaign directly to you on a weekly basis. You can also include a postcard that the recipient has to bring along with them at the time of the visit.

Regardless of the method that you choose, start small when you first begin testing. A small number would be somewhere in the range of 1,000 – 2,000 letters. A huge test would have somewhere around 5,000. Test your tracking system beforehand so that you know that it works.

Testing is an ongoing process that should be repeated throughout your marketing campaign. Just because something works, doesn't mean that it can't work better. Keep refining your idea, adjusting your content, and improving your response rates.

What to Say
Obviously, content is an important feature of any direct mail piece. The first step is to decide specifically what you are going to promote. This can be one key service, such as dental prophy, or a range of services that you offer. It is surprising how many pet owners are not aware of all of the services that a veterinary hospital may offer. This is especially true if you have a unique service that other practices in your area don't have.

For example, if you offer laser surgery you might be surprised at the number of clients who would want this for their pets if they knew what it was and that you offered it. As an add-on for routine procedures or more complicated cases, a quality client is generally willing to pay extra for better care. The more specific you are, the easier it is to see the benefits of an improved response rate

Checklist for Direct Mail Marketing

1. Your mailing list is vital. It can't be said often enough. Your mailing list is the single most important factor of creating success. It must be specific, accurate, and current. One mailing list won't last you ten years. It must be refreshed often. People move, pets die, and situations evolve. If you are going to target new clients then you should enlist a broker and buy a list. If you are targeting existing clients, then you already own your list. Have your staff make corrections to addresses if you receive returned mail. This will save you money on wasted postage in the future. There is a direct correlation between number of times that you use your mailing list and your bank account balance.

2. Get them to open your mail: If you are like most people, you sort your mail over the top of a trashcan. Anything that looks uninteresting is thrown away. The secret to compelling someone to open your mail is that it must be relevant to them. Personalize your mail, include incentives that they can immediately see, and consider using an old-fashioned stamp on the envelope. Research indicates that people are more likely to toss metered mail because it feels like bulk. A return address is also important because people want to know whom their mail is coming from.

3. Your headline must be attention getting. This can be your biggest benefit, a shocking fact, an interesting fact, or a compelling statement. The majority of your time writing copy should be focused on creating a dynamite headline. A high quality, emotionally stirring graphic can be used in combination with it to add punch. You want to drive home your point about your benefits by clearly defining a problem that the pet owner may have. It doesn't have to be a realized problem, as long as you explain to the reader why. Avoid putting your name at the top of the letter. It is very tempting for veterinary practices to put all correspondence on a letterhead, but at this point, the reader could care less about who you are.

4. The value-laden benefit. You must be clear in explaining to the reader what is in in your deal for them. It is all about the client. People don't care much about you or what you do, except as it relates to their lives. You must be concise about why they need it or should want what you are offering. A simple test that you can perform is to count the number of "I"'s in your copy and the number of "you"'s. If you have more "I"'s than "you"'s then you have gotten it wrong. Make sure that you don't overwhelm them with technical jargon. Your benefit should be detailed using language that any layperson can understand. For example, don't call a spay an ovariohsyterectomy... call it a spay.

5. Create a conversation. Except for the technical jargon, you should write the same way that you would talk to a client. People like to converse with other people who are real and friendly. This letter not a university paper that will be graded on technical accuracy. Strive for warmth, openness, and a down-to-earth tone. Keep your sentences short and easy to read. Think about it this way: would you rather talk to your friend or would you rather stand up and give a speech to an audience? Pet owners are people who want to know that you can relate to their concerns. Show them that you care and that your interest goes well beyond the dollar amount that they spend.

6. Don't worry about creating long copy. Studies show that readership falls off at somewhere around 350 words, but then doesn't dip again until around 10,000 words. This means that if you can keep your reader engaged past the short 350 word count, then length doesn't really matter that much. As long as your copy isn't boring and it flows naturally, you should not have a problem with the length.

7. When to use advertorial style. Advertorial style is a technique used to make an advertisement look like an informative article. It combines an advertisement and an editorial piece. This is powerful because consumer research shows us that editorials are five times more likely to be read than an advertisement. The difference between the two is crucial. In an ad, you are trying to sell someone something, but in an editorial, you are trying to teach someone something. This makes an editorial more credible to a reader.

8. A word about the font. It is a mistake to use several different typestyles when creating your letter. It created distraction. Limit yourself to only two different types, and choose serif fonts. The

rules are a little different than if you are creating web copy. Serif fonts have curls on the letters that are attractive to the eye. Times New Roman is one example. It is also not a good idea to use all capital letters. This implies that you are "shouting" at the reader. You can emphasis to your headline by making it bold or italicizing specific points. What's the deal with all of these rules? If your letter is hard to look at, people won't read it. It is that simple, yet that important.

9. Sub headlines to create a visual break. Since people tend to skim through a letter, sub-headlines are a great way to make sure that you are getting your point across. Sub-headlines are a way for people to understand your message, even if they don't read all the way through the copy. By breaking up your paragraphs into easily identifiable sections, you create added visual interest. This easy technique helps to keep your reader, well, reading. If you spent some time drafting (and rejecting) headlines for your copy, then many of these ideas will work for sub-headlines. Just be sure that the information that follows is logical.

10. Use odd numbers. This may sound odd, but using non-round numbers lends an air of truth to your copy. Once again, consumer research shows us that an article titled "7 Ways to Keep Your Pet Tick Free" is more likely to be read than "10 ways to Keep Your Cat Flea Free".

11. The dreaded guarantee. Veterinarians hate guarantees, because of course, no one can pledge that a pet will get better. They are feared because what if you gave them and people actually took you up on them? You would be out of business, right? Not necessarily, it all depends on the type of guarantee that you offer. There are relatively harmless guarantees that you can offer that are satisfying to your clients. People value their time; so for example, you can have an on-time guarantee, where if the client has to wait more than ten minutes past the scheduled appointment time, they are given a freebie of some sort. This actually just reinforces the importance of good customer service.

12. If you are trying to sell a high priced service, then divide it up. People have to think long and hard before investing dollars into high priced services. For this reason, it is very difficult to sell them in one step. You must first educate as to the "what" of the service. This means being able to explain in detail what it is and why it is

important. Only once the client understands it, can you attempt to sell them on it. For the purpose of direct mail, this might be motivating your reader to go to your website to learn more.

13. Know your audience. When you write copy for direct mail, write to a single pet owner. Direct the wording of your letter as if that pet owner were the only one you were giving information. Know what type of profile your "A" list clients have, what their interest and problems are. Address these typical "problems" in your copy, but make them specific. If you are addressing their problems, they are more likely to respond to your solution.

14. The postscript. Include a postscript (p.s.) in your letter. It is almost always read and should reiterate your offer to the reader. Tell them again how beneficial your service is to them. If you have a definite call to action, be sure to also include it here.

Here are some additional tips to consider when creating your direct mail campaign:

- Give a free gift to increase the response rate
- Prove any claims with detailed evidence to add credibility
- Consider hiring a professional copywriter for your content
- Make your offer easy to see at first glance
- Consider placing a headline on the outside of the envelope
- State your geographical service area
- Include a call to action; tell your readers exactly what you want them to do
- Create a sense of urgency and deadline in your copy
- Separate your features and benefits, with an emphasis on benefits
- Include case studies and success stories
- Put yourself on the mailing list
- Plan and prepare enough mailings for three months at a time, outsourcing if you need to
- Put your website address on all mailing pieces
- Mail with stamps; it gets opened before metered mail
- Lumpy mail gets attention--it gets opened and it gets a good response
- Offer a guarantee
- Use free information, free samples and a free demonstration as added incentive

- Put testimonials at the top of the content

As technology evolves and people become more dependent on computer services, new innovative ways to accomplish your marketing goals become available. However, for the small veterinary practice, many of these techniques are not cost effective, or simply to intimidating to take on. Recorded voice sales messages, codes to access websites, and pre filled in contact forms are all designed to improve and track your response rate. Yet, they are not always 100% necessary to plan a powerful direct mail marketing campaign.

Old-fashioned direct mail marketing still works, it you are careful. As a busy veterinary practice owner, you need your dollars to work hard for you in the simplest way possible. As long as you give your campaign a lot of planning and forethought, you should be able to anticipate any problems that may arise. Be sure to thoroughly question any company that offers to be a "one stop shop" for all of your direct mail marketing needs. While they can be extremely helpful, you want to be sure that they understand the veterinary industry completely before you hand over a project.

Although we have barely begun to dig into all of the possibilities that can be realized through direct mail efforts, you should be well prepared to jump into the pond with the big fish. This time around, though, instead of creating a ripple, you are ready to make a big splas

Chapter 10
Yellow Page
Marketing

"Doing business without advertising is like winking at a girl in the dark.
You know what you are doing, but nobody else does."
— Steuart H. Britt

Yellow Page advertising is so common in the veterinary industry that almost every practice does it. In popularity, yellow page ads are right up there with sending vaccine reminders. Currently, veterinarians are ranked in the top seventeen percent of professionals that use this form of advertising.

With a massive distribution market that reaches 76% of American adults in an average month and an audience that is already primed to buy, it is no wonder that 88% of users go on to contact a business found inside these pages.

Despite all of these good and wonderful facts about Yellow Page advertising, there has been a downward spiral in the effectiveness of it. The fact is that in today's society (and certainly in years to come) the overwhelming trend is for people to look to the internet. When you combine this with the thousands of dollars that a practice can spend monthly on an ad, you have to wonder, "Is it worth it?"

Is It Worth It?
There is no standard answer for every veterinary practice. It depends on the area that you live in, how much competition that you have, the quality of your ads, and knowing how well it is working for you.
Due to the expense, Yellow Page advertising carries a big risk. Essentially, you are committed for a full 12 months, with no option for revising your ads, or cancelling if it becomes apparent that it is not working for you. Imagine spending $17,000 (the average cost per year for the Yellow Pages) on a piece of equipment that did not work and that you could not return.

There is no doubt that today's society thrives on digital media, and that Yellow Page advertising is "old-school". However, the fact remains that in some locales, the yellow pages are still heavily referenced when it comes to finding a veterinarian. And, there are some impressive statistics out there that clearly demonstrate the benefits of a successful Yellow Page campaign.

Start by evaluating your current Yellow Page ads, figuring out your Return on Investment (ROI), and making sure that you have strong ads that will stand out from the crowd.

Know Your Return on Investment

Is your Yellow Page ad working? The only way to answer this question is to know what your Return on Investment (ROI) is. By doing a little research and putting pen to paper, you can easily determine how effective this advertising really is.

As they say, "The proof is in the pudding". If your practice does not already collect information about how new clients have heard of your practice, start now. It is as simple as having the receptionist ask every new client when they book an appointment how they heard about you. Keep a journal at the front desk for them to record the information into.

An alternative method would be to include the question on your new patient registration sheet. The receptionist must still follow through to be sure that the information is recorded, but these sheets can be placed in a folder until they are reviewed. Over a period of one month, or several months, this will show you exactly how many people come through your door as a result of yellow page advertising.

Return on investment (ROI) is a simple calculation that tells you if your dollars are spent wisely. Here is how to figure this out:

Step 1: The first thing that you need to know is how much income was derived as a result of your Yellow Page ad. Using the information from your receptionists, or new client forms; add up the total that all clients referred from the yellow pages spent at your practice in a given period. As an example, let's say that you generated $40,000 in six months.

Step 2: The second thing that you need to know is how much you spent on Yellow Page advertising for the same period of time that you calculated your income for. In our example, we are going to say that if you spend $1,500 per month on your ad, then the total for six months would be $9,000.00, with no expenses for design).

Step 3: Now you can write your equation: ROI = ($40,000 - $9,000) divided by $9,000 multiplied by 100.

Step 4: Once you perform the calculation, you will see that in our example your hospital would have a 344% return on investment.
It is ideal to do this calculation for a period of twelve months, because all practices are busier during some months than they are during others. The bottom line is that if you have a negative or low return on investment, then your advertising campaign is eating into your net profit.

So, how much should you make? A minimum goal should be a three to one ratio, or a profit of $3 for every dollar spent. In some categories of business, the average is $6 of profit for every $1 spent. If you are not getting a satisfactory minimum return, then you should reconsider your advertising strategy.

Smart and Strong Yellow Page Advertising
Grab your yellow pages, open it up to the "Veterinarian" or "Veterinary Hospital" section, and take a close look at what you see. Do any of the ads really "pop" out at you? 95% of the ads, including yours, probably look the same, just varying sizes and color. Most Veterinarians worry more about the monthly budget and allow the Yellow Pages Company to design their ads. This creates weak, ineffectual ads that blend into the page.

Advertising representatives know that you need an attention getting ad. But, remember that they have to do the same thing for every other client that they sell space to. They can provide you with all types of valuable information on how ads influence purchases, how satisfied customers with the number and quality of advertisements in your category, and how often people use each category to locate a veterinarian.

Although this information can certainly be appreciated when planning your ad, you must remember that publishers collect it for one reason: to sell their advertising space. They may have good intentions, but their goal is to sell you as much advertising as they can, and maximize their own profit.

Sales representative recommendations are typically things like:

- Get a bigger ad
- Add color
- Use multiple category listings

Sometimes, their recommendations are right. Maybe you do need a bigger, color ad that is posted in more than one category. However, you should never let the sales representative direct your budget; only you can decide how much of an investment that you are willing to make. Know what you are going to do before the sales representative gets to your office. Focus on creating ads that are smart (because they yield a reasonable return on investment) and strong (because they get noticed, even if they are not the biggest ad on the page).

The Objective of Yellow Page Advertising

The first place to begin creating a smart and strong Yellow Page ad is to know the objective. What are you trying to accomplish? Who are you targeting?

While a few of your existing clients may use the Yellow Pages to look up your phone number, the vast majority of users are potential new clients. And what are these potential new clients doing when they grab the phone book? They are looking to make a phone call! You are trying to get that new person to call YOU.

If you realize that your sole objective of your Yellow Page ad is to generate new business, then you are able to design an ad that will motivate people to call you, and hopefully be the ONLY one that they call.

A Winning Yellow Page Ad

Knowing what attracts potential new clients to a veterinarian in the Yellow Pages is the secret sauce in this recipe. What exactly are they looking for? The parts of a winning ad include all of the following:

- Differentiation: visual impact and the sum of what makes you better or different from all of the other veterinary practices
- Affordability: an indication of value
- Quality of your service
- redibility: trust, honesty, and what makes your statement believable
- Location of office and hours of availability
- Contact information
- A warm and fuzzy feeling

Notice at the top of the list is differentiation. Your ad will never succeed if it is not noticed. Visual impact makes your ad distinctive. Take a look at what everyone else is doing, and *don't do it*. Over 50% of the time, the first ad noticed is the first ad that is called.

The majority of these ads lack visual impact because they are designed by the graphic artists that work for the Yellow Pages. The same pictures and layout are used over and over again, because these artists often have many ads to do over the course of a day. Here are some simple ways to ad visual impact:

Include warm & fuzzy photographs or pictures (emotion evoking graphic images that have not already been seen in an advertisement)

- Borders
- White space
- A different font

Regardless of whatever you choose to do, at the end of the day your ad must be distinctive, unique, and in contrast to the other ads on the page.

Given the considerable expense of Yellow Page advertisements, it is advisable considering hiring the best graphic artist that you can find to create your ad. This does not mean that you should hire the kid who is good with Photoshop on his computer.

This means that you should invest the time to seek out a professional artist. Although this will cost you more money in the short term, it is well worth the investment. Remember, you are committed to twelve months of advertising, so make it meaningful.

Differentiation also includes the sum of what makes you better or different from all of the other veterinary practices. There has to be something that sets you apart from your competitors. Again, look at what the other practices in your area are saying in their ad.

Try to identify an area of your practice that can provide a solution to a client's needs and wants, in a way that has not already been defined and filled by someone else. This information can be used in both your headline and the body of your ad.

The Anatomy of a Yellow Page Ad

A Yellow Page ad is made up of multiple parts that fit together in a cohesive way. In other words, your ad should flow and make sense to a reader quickly. People do not want to spend hours making phone calls and trying to gather information. You must make it simple for them.

Here are the components of an ad:

- Attention grabbing, benefit laden headline
- A fantastic, emotion-evoking photograph
- A body that includes the benefits of calling you
- Contact information with a strong call to action

The Attention Grabbing Headline

As you are reviewing those ads in the Yellow Pages, what type of headline do you see? Most likely, it is the name and logo of the business. Consider the importance of that as it relates to your objective. Are you selling your name, or are you selling a service? People do not care about who you are.

Veterinarians sell a public service, so your headline should clearly communicate the service and the benefits that a client will receive from that service.

- Run your headline big and bold across the top of your ad
- Your headline must grab the reader attention and compel them to read more
- Focus on the FELT NEEDS of pet owners
- Use "you", and "your pet"; Do NOT use "we" or "I" (Remember it is all about what motivates them)
- Decide on a style
    - Create emotional appeal and speak to a pet owners bond with their pet
    - Use expert appeal by pointing out your extensive experience and that you have a high rate of satisfaction and success
    - Fear appeal is highly effective. Consider an editorial style. Studies show us that people read editorial material over advertising material at a rate of six to one.
    - If you have a Unique Selling Proposition, use it (See the example for the all-inclusive facility)
    - Humor appeal is not often used in the veterinary industry, but it can be a great way to grab your reader's attention and make your ad memorable. If you are creative enough to think of a funny situation that you can create a witty saying around, people will notice it.

"LAW OF CAT INERTIA"
"A cat at rest will tend to remain at rest, unless acted upon by some outside force, such as the opening of cat food, or a nearby scurrying mouse."

An example of an attention getting headline might be any of the following:

"Warning: Don't Call Any Veterinary Practice Until You Read This!"

"Discover what the American Animal Hospital Association is and how a certified practice can have a tremendous impact on the quality of your pet's care"

"Discover California's First State of the Art Veterinary Center, All-Inclusive Luxury Pet Resort and Spa"
"You owe it to your pet to learn about Evergreen Animal Care Center… the place where convenience for you and caring for your pet come together"

"With over 20 Years of quality service and 1,000's Of happy, healthy pets"

"You can be assured that your pet will receive compassionate and quality care at an affordable price… it's our promise"

"You're Pets… Our Family"
"Your pet is more than just another dog or cat; they are an integral part of your family unit.
Visit the experts and see that delivering superior healthcare is not just our job, it is our standard"

The Graphic Image
Graphic Image

Many veterinary practices choose to use their logo as the main image, but this can be a mistake. The style of the graphic image that you choose should correlate with the headline and type of advertising appeal that you have chosen.

Due to the nature of the human-companion animal bond, emotional appeals are probably the easiest and most relevant form that veterinary advertising can take. Photographs or images of pets that evoke strong emotion are an easy way to jump out at people, since pets are a highly passionate subject already.

The position of the graphic in the ad is also very important. You want to put your picture on the left side of ad, because people read from left to right. Placing your ad on the right side will draw their eyes directly to the picture and they may end up missing your content. And, be sure the photo faces into your ad, and not into a competitor ad.
A word of caution about photographs and graphics... use only ONE unique graphic element that grabs the eye. Too many visual images will clutter up your ad and take away from your message.

A Body That Includes Benefits, Benefits, and More Benefits
Clients have choices about where they spend their pet health care dollars. What are the benefits that a client gains when they choose your practice? Ask yourself what your average client gains from you that they can't get from your competitor.

It should be something that is client or pet centered, and not something that is a benefit to you. For example, you may have a beautiful building, which most certainly is an important part of your marketing efforts, but the client is not buying your building... they are buying the service that you provide. Clients care about what they are getting out of their interaction with you.

For example:
- "Our in-house board certified surgeons and specialists mean that we will rarely have to refer your pet to another facility for advanced care. You will find that our rates are lower, or comparable to that of other specialists."
- "We provide you substantial value for your dollar. We package most of our services into affordable bundles. If you compare the services

we include with the service of other hospitals, you will find that we offer you a big savings!"

Figure out what your practice's strongest selling point is by knowing what pet owners in your area will care about the most.

A Call to Action

An often overlooked part of print advertising is the call to action. It is an advertising concept that leads a potential client to take action. The theory is that if you tell people what you want them to do; they are more likely to do it.

A strong call to action near your telephone number is an absolute must. Give them a reason to call and tell them to call you. It can be as simple as "Call Us Today!", or you can be creative about including extra bonus incentives to drive telephone calls.

This can be a free gift, an informative report ("Five Questions to Help You Choose the Right Veterinarian for Your Pet"), or any other bonus that you can imagine.

A call to action can also be used to drive people to visit your website. For example, "Visit http://www.myanimalhospital.com to download your FREE pet health report today!" is an example of Education-Based Marketing. You should be somewhat familiar with this concept, as Veterinarians, drug manufactures and product vendors do this all of the time.

How best to sell that box of heartworm preventative? Educate pet owners about the disease! How can you increase the number of dental prophy performed in your practice? Educate pet owners about dental disease! Through education you build credibility and rapport; therefore your sales offer is trustworthy. The client understands the need and knows how to take action.

Client Testimonials

One of the best forms of promotion, and a true advertising workhorse is client testimonials. They are a powerful way to immediately increase your credibility, and establish trust, honesty, and what makes you believable. Research shows that people's attitudes are directly and indirectly influenced by other people's opinions and expectations. Testimonial advertising takes advantages of a person's basic need to identify with others. And, it works.

Truth in advertising laws aside, it must be done ethically. Testimonial advertising is governed by the American Veterinary Medical Association's (AVMA) code of ethics. According to the ethics code, Testimonials or endorsements are statements that are intended to influence attitudes regarding the purchase or use of products or services. It further states:

- "Testimonials or endorsements are advertising, and they should comply with the guidelines for advertising. In addition, testimonials and endorsements of professional products or services by veterinarians are considered unethical unless they comply with the following: "
- The endorser must be a bonafide user of the product or service.
- There must be adequate substantiation that the results obtained by the endorser are representative of what veterinarians may expect in actual conditions of use.
- Any financial, business, or other relationship between the endorser and the seller of a product or service must be fully disclosed.

Does Size Really Matter?

We have all heard that bigger is not necessarily better, but is this true for yellow page ads? Well, sometimes. The larger that your ad is, the more likely that it will be seen. Bigger ads also tend to get better placement inside the book. But there is not a lot of benefit to just increasing the size of your ad without considering other alternatives. Fortunately, your ad does not have to be the biggest ad in the Yellow pages to be effective. Along with the overall design, placement can play an even more important role than size does.

Of course, the larger your ad, the more information you can include on it. The total overall size though, should really depend on your advertising budget and placement. Buy the smallest ad that you can that will accomplish your goals, (unless you can afford that giant ad.... Then by all means go for it!)

Show the sales representative where you would like your ad to be placed based on the size that you are considering. Sometimes you will be able to move to a better position, for relatively little change in cost, by making your ad larger. Or, you may be able to reduce expenses by making your ad a little smaller, without compromising position.

Regardless of what the sales representative may tell you, the placement of your ad can be more important than the size of your ad. However, the size of your ad can effect placement. Make sure that the ad that you purchase will not be printed on the inside fold of the book. Irregular shapes, such as a dollar bill sized ad, or a 3/8s page ad will almost never be placed on the inside fold.

So, what is the big deal about being on the inside fold? That is usually the last place that a reader will look, and you can lose as much as 50% of the readership. That equals 50% of potential new clients who will not look at your ad!

Should the Ad Be In Color?
Adding color can almost double the cost of Yellow Page advertisement. Is it worth it? It depends on your ad. A well designed black and white ad can be more effective than a poorly designed color ad. Although it is nice, color is far less important than the ad itself and your placement. An effective ad will pull the reader to the content.

When considering ad design and whether or not to use color, it is imperative to remember that your ad also reflects the quality of your service. The nicer that your ad is, the better the image is that you will project. If your budget allows for color, then by all means go for it. However, the use (or nonuse) of color will not make or break your ad campaign.

Other Tips
- Use ONLY serif typeface fonts. It is faster to read and can actually increase the readers comprehension
- Bad sentence structure, poor capitalization and punctuation, bolding, and italics are also no-nos. This can drastically reduce comprehension levels by as much as 50%
- Don't use medical jargon. Use terms and words that a lay person can understand
- A smaller ad should have only one single focus and one solution for a problem
- Use #12 font size for the ad copy, or #14 if your demographics include older people
- Be sure to list all of your contact information
- Make sure that your white page listings are correct
- ASK for a PROOF... mistakes are costly and the publisher will not be liable for them

- Your yellow page advertising is the first impression your business makes. It should make you look honest, reliable, smart, and professional.
- If your ad is large enough, list every product or service that represents five percent your services in your ad. List any product or service that you believe has the potential to become five percent or more of your service
- If your ad is not large enough, do not overwhelm it by trying to cram every single piece of information about your practice. Keep it focused.

Tracking the Success of your Yellow Page Ad
Did you know that out of all of the veterinary practices that utilize Yellow Page advertising, only 27% of them actually tract the effectiveness of their ads?
In order for you to make informed decisions about future ads, you must be able to track and calculate your return on investment. If you have multiple ads under multiple heading, be sure to ask what page of the phone book they found your ad on.

Test Your Ad
The design and layout concepts discussed in this report are easily adapted to work as newspaper advertisements. If you take the time to create a few different Yellow Page ads well in advance of the deadline, you can test your ads by running them for a week in your local newspaper. Create different headlines, graphics, and appeals for each ad. Track the ads carefully and you will be able to determine which ad generates the highest number of calls. The top performing ad would be the one that you would want to commit to a Yellow Page advertisement.

Which Directory Should You Choose?
With so many different directories available to choose from, which one should you allocate your advertising dollars to?

The three main types of Yellow Page directories are your phone companies, regional, and local. While all of these directories get used by someone, it is important to find out which one is used the most. Ask your friends, staff, and family which directory they most commonly use.
Here are some other considerations:

- Which publisher's phonebook contains the real residential white pages? That book will be on the top of the phonebook pile in most homes and businesses.
- To start with, budget your ad to appear in the most widely used directory. Purchase the correct size ad space. Do not try to save money by cutting your ad size and placement so that you can run an extra ad someplace else.
- 62% of people use the large, regional directory
- 38% of people use the small, local directory

Questions for your sales representative:
- How widely is it used? Who says so, and can they prove it?
- Is it distributed to every home and business?
- What market coverage does the book offer?

Ask For Discounts

Although discounting policies will vary by publisher, most of them will have some type of discounting program to offer you. Deep discounts can be had if you are willing to work a little for them.

Tell your sales representative that you have decreased your advertising budget and will be decreasing the amount of advertising that you do with them. Ask for their lowest rates, and don't forget about deals for listing under multiple headings, ad size, and color versus black and white.

Although they will be anxious to close a sale, do not be pressured into signing a contract. Often, the longer that you wait, the better the deal becomes. Let your sales representative know that they should contact you when you are closer to making a decision.

If you are a new advertiser, insist on a substantial discount if you are a new advertiser, and track the effectiveness of the ad to see if you want to pay full price next year. Often, you can get your ad price cut in half for the first year.

Watch Out For Fraud

When you receive an invoice for Yellow Page advertising, make sure that it is a real invoice, and not a solicitation. Many businesses are getting caught in a scam where alternative, or fake, directories send a business an invoice that looks like a Yellow Page invoice. It is in fact a solicitation, even though they may claim an affiliation with your local phone company, use the familiar "walking fingers" logo, and feature the name "Yellow Pages".

If you receive a bill FOR Yellow Page advertising, check for a disclaimer somewhere on the invoice that sates "THIS IS NOT A BILL. THIS IS A SOLICITATION AND YOU ARE UNDER NO OBLIGATION TO PAY THE AMOUNT STATED ABOVE UNLESS YOU ACCEPT THIS OFFER".

The confusion arises because the "walking fingers" logo and the name "Yellow Pages" are not protected by a federal trademark, copyright, or trademark registration. However, there is no connection between alternative directories and the well-known Yellow Pages.
Other things that you can do to protect yourself are:
o   Ask for a copy of the previous directory edition
o   Ask the publisher for written information such as distribution figures, method of distribution, and the directories life span
o   Ask if the directories are free, and if there is a fee, how much they are
o   Call your local Yellow Pages and ask them if the directory is affiliated with them

Although it is risky, Yellow Page advertising can be a great way to close the circuit in your marketing mix. If you have done a thorough job creating interest in your practice though other mediums, then you want people to be able to find you in the yellow pages.

Make no mistake, every single element of your ad counts in a major way. If it is done well, it can be a profitable investment, but if it is done poorly you are committed to throwing your money away. It can be beneficial to consider not only hiring a graphic artist, but also an advertising professional that can copy write the headline and body of your ad.

Allow plenty of time to organize and plan your Yellow Page advertising strategy. This is not something that should be rushed into on short notice, but instead methodically planned over a period of months, if possible. By taking the time and expending the effort to do it well, your Yellow Pages ad can give you a satisfying return for years to come.

Chapter 11
Mobile Marketing

Have you been struggling to sell services and grow your practice? If so, you're not alone. Veterinary visits and over all practice profits are declining. Bayer recently published a study to reveal what impact the economy has had on the veterinary profession. The findings showed that 55% of practices saw a decrease in the number of patient visits, and another 15% reported that growth was flat, with no movement in any direction at all.

In addition, Veterinarians have the lowest profit margins when compared to other professionals such as CPAs, dentists, chiropractors, and optometrists, and therapists. (Forbes.com, 2010). Less than 10% of the income that is generated translates into actual profit.

This fact brings us full circle back to the effectiveness of marketing your veterinary practice. If your revenue is stagnant or declining, then it is more important than ever to re-evaluate your strategy. Do you need to do more marketing, or so you simply need better marketing? Well, that really depends on what you are already doing and whether or not you are seeing results. Sometimes it is beneficial to explore new avenues of promoting your practice, and take a fresh look at where your dollars are being spent.

If you're' sitting their scratching your head and wondering what you could possibly do that hasn't been done a thousand times already, here is a new platform worth considering: mobile web marketing.

You may be thinking, "That's great, but what the heck is it and how do I do it, and while we are on the subject, how much is it going to cost me?" Mobile web marketing is the process of marketing to clients through their cell phone.

It uses both advertising and promotional techniques to generate business for your practice. The target is both new clientele and existing clientele, depending on the techniques that are used. Mobile web marketing can be simple and cost effective too.

How Does It Work?

If you haven't yet discovered the world of smart phones and the convenience of mobile web, don't be intimidated. It works in much the same way as the old standby desktop internet, but is designed for a cell phone's smaller screens, keyboard, and for use without a mouse.

The easiest way to look at this is to consider your website. Unless converted for viewing on a mobile device, your regular website won't work well.

There are too many things, like HTML tags, that clutter it up. This makes it hard for someone to view it, hard for them to navigate it, and generally a hassle for the user. This lowers the chances that someone will spend any time at all viewing your business or requesting information about your services.

Do you really need mobile web marketing?

Well, consider the fact that mobile web is poised to be bigger than desktop internet usage ever was. There are 4.8 billion mobile phone users, compared to just 1.7 billion desktop internet users. The implications of this massive reach mean that there is a larger base – almost four times larger, in fact- in which to actively market to.

Think about the business that you may use that have already begun to tap this market. Banks now offer mobile banking. Airlines offer mobile alerts and mobile check in. Other large companies use the mobile web for sending out news updates. Social media, such as Facebook and Twitter, have also attracted a large numbers of mobile users.

Compelling Proof

The mobile web-marketing concept is big enough that it has garnered the attention of industry giants. In February 2010, Google announced that they are changing their creation strategy to focus on mobile first. They will then adapt their creations for use on desktop computers. They have seen a 500% growth in mobile web use between the years of 2008-2010, and a 67% increase in the number of mobile web searches performed.

> In North America, there is an average of 110% growth in mobile web usage each year. This translates into 1.3 % of all web page views come from a cell phone.

Is there science behind this trend? Massive consumer surveys tell marketers that this is a way to increase a business's bottom line: to generate more sales. Kantar Media's Complete preformed an extensive survey of 2010 Smartphone users.

The findings showed that:
- More users will call a business based on search results. In fact, 1/3 of them will call or visit the business that they find on local searches.

- One in three Android and iPhone users discovered at least two new businesses during the first quarter of the survey.

- The most sought after information included a business address, phone number, and more information on what that business does.

Not only that, but mobile users are three times more likely to make a purchase. This is because when someone does a local search using their mobile phone, they are usually already looking to buy. It eliminates a step in the consumer buying cycle. The best part is that it also reaches multiple age ranges, instead of a narrower demographic.

Survey Your Clients and Know Your Market

To get an idea if mobile web marketing will benefit your practice right away, consider talking to your top spending clients. Hopefully, you know who these people are and you have developed a good rapport with them.

One important thing, though. Don't just ask anyone and everyone about their mobile usage. Narrow your focus to your ideal clients. These are the ones who already spend money with you. By knowing what is important to these people, you can attract more... just like them.

Ask these A list clients what type of cell phone they use and how they use it. Do they surf the web, look up businesses, use text messaging, and access their Facebook accounts? What kind of information would they find useful? What would they like to see you sending them? By compiling this information, you are able to determine what type of marketing will be worth pursuing and where to direct the bulk of your effort.

Getting an early start on this savvy marketing technique will put you one step ahead of your competition. While 92% of veterinary hospitals may have traditional websites, few of them have made the transition to mobile web. This is a golden opportunity to explore a new marketing platform that is literally exploding in popularity.

Getting In On the Mix

There is more than one way to advertise and promote using mobile web.

- Mobile Website – serves to help people find you and your services. It is most useful for local searches, but there is no limit to the creative way that you can use it. Consider features that make your client's life easier. Booking appointment, medication refills and orders, posting coupons, and other client-based services could be included.

- SMS advertising- serves to promote a service or product in a way that leads to a sale. SMS stands for "short message service". It is the technology that you see whenever you send or receive a text message. There are services that can provide location based broadcasting, Bluetooth broadcasting, and more. This is great for short health alerts, and pet health issues in the news. For example, "A Horse in Eastern Tennessee was found to have a fatal case of West Nile Virus! Call us today to schedule an appointment for a life saving vaccine!"

- MMS is similar to SMS, but allows for images, videos, and sound to be included. The inclusion of audio and graphics allows for a richer media message that SMS alone, thereby increasing the likelihood that it will be noticed.

- In game marketing takes advantage of the popularity of mobile gaming. Key advertisements are placed inside of the game. There are pet themed mobile games and applications in use. Since veterinary practices tend to be limited by their physicality, this is probably not a practice means of generating targeted leads.

- Targeted ad placements using the major content providers – Google, Yahoo, and others- have numerous programs designed to display your ads on relevant sites. They also offer valuable reporting tools so that tracking the efficacy of your marketing dollars is easy.

- Social media is another are in mobile web that has been experiencing astronomical growth. If your practice has a social media site (and it should), then you can also incorporate this into a mobile web marketing campaign.

- Direct mail marketing via the mobile web is another option that is both effective and can save money. It works in a similar fashion like traditional direct mailings, but is delivered to a cell phone instead of a mailbox.

A core benefit to these techniques is that users must opt in and they can opt out at anytime. This ensures that your promotional message never winds up in the trash bin. Your subscribers actually want to her what you are offering. The cost varies depending on different factors, such as whether you do it yourself or hire someone else. For the purpose of this report, we are going to focus on the two things that are the easiest for veterinary hospitals to implement: a mobile website and SMS marketing.

Tips for Success
Regardless of the technique that you choose, there are some tips that universally apply to all mobile web marketing.

- Keep it client focused. When you are thinking about what you want to include, remember that it has to be based on the desires of your clients. Include the things that are useful to pet owners. For example, they probably won't care about how many square feet your building is, or that you have a Super-Tech 3000 Ultrasonic Scaler, but they will care if you offer them ½ off on $25 gift certificates during the month of November... just in time for Christmas.

- Keep it simple. Write text that is short, simple, and to the point. Be direct so that clients don't have to wade through a river of words to find out what they need to know. Simply state who you are, what you do, and what your competitive advantage is. Avoid long or complicated forms, as people are not likely to take the time to fill them out.

- Keep it fast. The key to mobile web is that it is easy to use and FAST. It is a mistake to include complicated graphics, animations, or videos. While you may think that the little dog running around on the screen is cute, many users will find it annoying, and it slows down the flow of information.

- Don't forget to test it out. Whether you have an ad or mobile website, test it on different cell phones to see how it looks. Since different phones have different graphic displays, your media might not look right on some devices. If you discover a problem, you can address it correctly.

- Track your mobile website traffic. Google analytics is a free tool that tells you exactly how many people are viewing your mobile website and what they are clicking on. The information is useful because it will allow you to tweak things in order to increase traffic.

- Choose simple domain names for your mobile website. The shorter and more relevant it is, the easier it is to remember and navigate to.

Making a Mobile Website
If you want to launch a mobile website quickly and for minimal cost, there are very good resources available on the internet to help you do this. For less than you will spend on dinner tonight, you can create your new mobile website. It is as simple as a tool that will automatically optimize your current website for viewing on a cell phone. Some of these cost less than $10!

There are also other alternatives for creating a mobile website, such as templates that allow you to just plug in your custom information. If you are into doing things in a big way, there are certified mobile web developers available for hire. Award winning mobile websites have a few things in common.

You can save yourself some aggravation by making sure they are built into your site from the beginning.

- Include an icon that allows a viewer to switch back and forth between your regular website and your mobile website. This contributes to the sense of being simple to use. If a client accidently goes to your regular site on their mobile phone, they can easily change over.

- Consider that most people will use the mobile web while they are on the go. This means that they need to find you fast, and they need to be able to instantly see the information they need. One fantastic way to do this is to make your telephone number a "click to call" link. That way they can effortlessly call your practice anytime.

- Remember the top things that people are looking for when using a mobile device: your practice address, phone number, business hours, and relevant information such as what you do and what products you sell.

It is critical that you have a clear vision for what you want your mobile website to do. In general, it should do four things:

- Introduce your veterinary service and what you do

- Show them where you are

- Drive them to call you or come in

- Encourage them to sign up for your newsletter, SMS, or MMS promotions if you have them

All of this should be accomplished in as few words as possible, often with less than 100. Mobile users simply do not take the time to read much of what is written. They are looking for specific information, and if you don't give it to them, then they may decide it is easier to find someone else who will.

Promotional Ideas
Once you have your website up and running, don't forget that you need to promote it. Here are some easy ways to do this:

- Advertise
    1. Promotional materials, such as brochures, handouts, and invoices
    2. List it on your regular website
    3. Print it on your business cards
    4. Consider telling the press; mobile marketing is still new enough that a small business launching a mobile site is considered newsworthy

- Promotional ideas
    1. Run a mobile only special. For example, give mobile users a secret code that entitles them to a 25% discount on an annual wellness plan for their dog.
    2. Hold a prize drawing that requires mobile users to enter their name or number for a chance to win.
    3. A contest is another great way to spread the word, like having the first ten users who can correctly answer a few pet health questions wins a free dental care kit. You could even tie this in with your other dental promotions, and double up on your educational message.
    4. Send out coupons to mobile users only. Again, you can create a special code that they use at checkout to receive a discount on their bill.

SMS and MMS Messaging

SMS is most likely the most popular form of mobile marketing right now. It is simple, it doesn't require special phone for viewing, and any veterinary practice can do it. It has the potential for reaching the most number of users during any given campaign.

In fact, you may already own a valuable tool that you are not utilizing. Many veterinary management software programs have a built-in capability to send out appointment reminders and vaccine reminders via text messaging. So many practices have great software features, but fail to use them. It makes sense to use what you have, so spend some time investigating.

Even if your program has become a bit dated, the top ones usually offer online updates. If you decide not to do SMS / MMS marketing, you should still update your management software on a regular basis. Oth-

erwise, you may miss enhanced features and critical patches that re-
solve problems.

Check with the technical support team of your management software
company and find out.

Advantages:

- Reach a large market without spending a lot

- Schedule delivery during day time hours so clients are not disturbed
  at night by your messages

- Encourage more frequent visits to both your location and your websites

- Builds a relationship with clients outside of the visit

Like the country great Willie nelson once said, "You're always on my
mind." Frequent contact keeps your clients thinking about you, and
consumer studies tell us that the more often they think of you, the
more likely they are to visit you. This is what brand awareness is all
about.

Do Something Old in a New Way
Virtually every veterinary hospital in America sends out vaccine reminder cards and calls to remind clients of upcoming appointments.
Some even send out reminders for geriatric wellness and blood work
(For chronic long-term conditions that are medicated, such as thyroid
conditions, managing organ failure patients, those on NSAIDS, and
much more).

Few practice owners realize what the true cost of this is, and how much
they actually recoup using these old methods. Even less know what the
compliance rate is.

The benefits of using SMS for appointment and vaccine reminders are
centered on the fact that it will save you money. Consider the following:

- The amount of money that you spend purchasing reminder cards

- The amount of money that you spend on postage

- The amount of printer ink used and staff time creating, printing, and mailing cards

- How often your cards are returned in the mail and never get seen by the client

- How much money you spend on the staff that make those telephone calls

- How much the telephone usage costs you in term of calls outside of your local area code

While any and all of these things are a great argument for implementing text messaging in your practice, you can also think about the things that you may consider incidental, but are important to your clients.

- Announcing when you are closing early, or closed, because of the holidays and other events

- Announcing extended hours or other changes that affect when your clients will have access to you

- Letting a client know about changes that could influence your bond with them, such as when you are out of town and will have a relief doctor working.

While all of these possibilities are great ways to connect with your clients, there is an ever-greater potential for using this as a means of increasing your sales and compliance rates. That way is through using SMS as an active medium for running promotions.

Do People Really Want This?
President Obama did it, Pizza Hut does it, Coca Cola does it, as well as other major companies such as Jiffy Lube, Best Buy, and Ashley Furniture. Since clients must choose to receive information from you in this manner, you can almost guarantee increased compliance.

Unlike traditional mail and email, text messages are always read. There is no such thing as spam. It is also incredibly easy to see when your message was delivered, and when it was opened. In the United States, an average of three billion text messages is sent and received EVERY DAY.

Just like any of your other marketing efforts, you must offer incentives for clients to opt in. Reward them for using the service, and make sure it is something that will motivate them to join. Consider adding a section to your client registration form that has a box to check if they would like to receive text messages from your office, and clearly outline what the incentive for doing so is.

The Anatomy of SMS
Your text messages must be compelling and short. It is realistic to expect that you need to motivate your clients in 160 words or less. This sounds hard, but really, it is just a matter of being direct. For example, if you want to promote your microchip service, you might say the following:

> "Microchip event on Monday, 4:00 to 6:00 PM November 4! Deep Discounts! Protect your companion. One in every five dogs become lost and never find their way home again. Don't be a statistic: a microchip offers your pet safety and security. ABC Veterinary Hospital wants to help! Call (your linked phone number) or visit (your mobile site) to reserve a spot for your dog. Space is limited!"

The most important two parts are the message and the call to action. The message should be compelling and have a clear call to action. This is why it is a good idea to use a mobile website and SMS as complimentary campaigns. Without a mobile website, your clients are still likely to try to access your website from their mobile phone, but may become frustrated if it is difficult to view. They may end up not using the service you are promoting, because you have made it too difficult for them to do so.

Once you have a built a list of clients who opt-in, do a test run. A wonderful way to test whether or not SMS will work for you is to consider a trial run. Pick a rainy day when you know that business will be slow, and send out an incredible coupon offer that is good for that day only. It may wind up being the difference between losing money that day and at least being able to pay your staff wages.

MMS versus SMS

MMs has a powerful advantage over SMS in that it allows you to include images, graphics, sound clips, and video to your presentation, along with text. It is commonly referred to "rich" content because it allows the viewer to be immersed in visual and audio experience. Physiologically, it provides a visual and/or audio connection to your message. It tends to have a bigger impact because it uses multiple senses to effect someone's perception.

As you probably already know, the decision to purchase veterinary services is heavily influenced by emotions. The human companion animal bond is the number one most important factor for creating a demand. This is why graphics and images are so commonly a part of the marketing process. MMS allows you to send a marketing message that let's your clients "feel" it. Simple text messages simply do not have the same potential for impact.

The disadvantage is that you most likely cannot do this yourself. Creating dynamic MMS messages is beyond the capability of most veterinary practices. Another consideration is the way it can look on different phones. A message that is perfect for a Blackberry may not look so hot on a lesser cell phone. This doesn't mean it is out of your reach. Many companies out there specialize in this type of marketing.

Conclusion
As you can see, the opportunity for marketing a veterinary practice isn't limited by what you have always known or always done. As technology expands, so does the chance of utilizing techniques that promote your practice in cheaper and more efficient ways.

When budgeting for these newer methods, realize that you don't necessarily have to increase your existing budget. If you take the time to review the other means by which you advertise, you may find that you can cut back on things that aren't working.

For example, yellow page ads are hard to track, and usage decreases every day. By reducing and revamping these ads, you may discover that you have extra money that you can channel into these new avenues. If you stop sending "snail mail" reminders, then the money that you save in postage can be put towards developing a mobile website. Be creative when looking for way to allocate advertising money towards mobile marketing.

Above all, don't be afraid to reach out and try in new and innovative ways. As the economic world of the veterinary industry is changing, you may find it easier to be flexible and adapt. The great thing about marketing is that if you decide that you don't like what you are doing, it is easy to move on to something else.

If you'd like to find out more about our own mobile marketing packages and how they can be tailored to your veterinary practice, visit www.vetnetmarketing.com/mobile.

Conclusion

We hope this book acts as as a catalyst to get you moving forward with your own marketing plan. Technologies will continue to change in the coming years, but the focus will still be the same - connect with your clients and give lots of value! Different online services may come and go, but the fundamentals of building relationships with your customers will never change. I suggest that you take these strategies (both online and offline) and implement one or two at a time.

Start with email marketing. This is the one key strategy that you need to implement right away. Your veterinary practice is wasting money every day if you don't have a system for capturing names and email addresses when visitors come to your site.

Build a blog that provides solid content using video. Keep your clients informed about the latest changes; offer health and nutrition tips each week. Take a lesson from Jim the realtor or Gary the wine expert. Host a weekly video show. Give good solid content that will keep people coming back again and again. The point is to implement something.

We host a small business marketing workshop in our home town of Knoxville each month. We throw out a bunch of ideas during these two hour groups and at the end of each meeting, we find that many of the members are both excited and overwhelmed at the same time. Sometimes giving people too much information at one time isn't the best approach. Think back to my point in the book when we talked about the "Power of One" in terms of Web sites. As the saying goes, you eat an elephant one bite at a time. Start with one strategy.

If you don't have the time or feel you still lack the "know how" to implement some of these online strategies, don't let it stop you from moving forward. Hire it out! It will be the best investment you've ever made for your practice.

At VetNet Marketing, we specialize in implementing all of these marketing systems into our client's practice. We realize that you as a veterinarian only have so much time, and that time needs to be spent on what you do best- taking care of your client's beloved pets.

This book is not meant to be complex. It's meant to give an overview of resources for branding you or your practice online. Our intent is not to bog you down in too much detail, but to show you how powerful these strategies can be applied to your own practice.

If you have questions or would like a free 30 minute marketing consultation on how these strategies can be tailored to your own veterinary practice, call us today at 866-724-0355 or email us through our contact page at www.VetNetMarketing.com.

About the Authors

VetNet Marketing is a marketing company located in Knoxville, TN. We specialize in helping veterinarians create and implement marketing systems that attract qualified prospects and clients top their practice. These strategic systems are based on time-tested principles of online and offline direct response marketing and are tailored specifically to veterinary industry.

Jonathan Taylor
Jonathan Taylor is a professional marketing consultant and author of the book *The Official Small Business Guide to Marketing 2.0*. For years Jonathan has worked with small businesses, teaching them more effective, yet inexpensive ways to promote their products and services both online and offline. Jonathan is president of the *Knoxville Marketing Meetup*, Knoxville's largest small business meetup organization.

He and Russell Portwood host a popular online radio show every Saturday morning that teaches listeners how to better market their business online.

Russell Portwood
Russell placed his first site on the internet in 1997 – a long time ago in web time. Since then, he has sold digital products and services as well as physical products using the www as a marketing tool. His real passion is in helping others use the power of digital marketing to reach their business goals. Russell and Jonathan have taught beginners (and some old timers as well) how to start their own profitable online businesses through their site BeginnerInternet Business.com. A teacher and coach, Russell bases his success on the success of others.

Now, veterinarians everywhere have a unique opportunity to capitalize on the knowledge and experience of Russell and Jonathan to catapult their practices to new levels. Combining solid marketing practices (that actually work) with the power of internet marketing, vets everywhere will reach new heights in profits and personal satisfaction.

Made in the USA
Lexington, KY
26 October 2012